THE DESERT AND THE SOWN

The Desert and the Sown

NOMADS IN THE WIDER SOCIETY

CYNTHIA NELSON, Editor

Institute of International Studies
University of California, Berkeley

Standard Book Number 0-87725-121-5
Library of Congress Card Catalog Number 73-620208

PREFACE

By chance, during the academic year 1971-1972, several anthropologists specifically interested in nomadism were living in the Middle East, and were teaching courses and/or doing research on issues related to nomad-sedentary interaction in the Middle Eastern area. As chairperson of the Department of Sociology-Anthropology at The American University in Cairo at that time, I suggested to the administration that an international conference be held in Cairo to discuss the dynamic processes relating nomads and sedentaries in the Middle East. I appreciatively acknowledge the enthusiastic response and generous support of The American University in hosting this international conference.

The main purpose of the conference was to bring together anthropologists who had recently done fieldwork in the Middle East and North Africa in order to discuss the relationships between pastoralists and non-pastoralists, as opposed to the usual procedure of merely providing ethnographic descriptions of particular pastoral/nomadic groups. The conference took place in March 1972 at The American University in Cairo, with participants from Egypt, the Sudan, Saudi Arabia, Lebanon, Tanzania, England, Norway, and the United States. The conference was planned and organized with the cooperation of Talal Asad, British Academy Visiting Fellow on leave from Hull University, and Donald Cole, Assistant Professor of Anthropology at The American University in Cairo.

It is a characteristic of Middle Eastern nomadic communities that they are closely involved with a wider society; that they interact with cultivators, traders, administrators, and men of religion; that they depend for their livelihood, directly or indirectly, on economic and political institutions whose centers generally lie beyond their immediate vicinity; and that they share a language and a religion with a population which extends far beyond their area of residence. These facts have seldom been adequately dealt with by anthropologists, however. Indeed, although many authors warn us that nomads (generally equated with tribesmen) must be seen in relation to the greater social and cultural world of Islam and to the national and regional political and economic spheres of which they are parts, they generally proceed to discuss nomadic groups as if they were in fact well-bounded social and cultural units, capable of standing on their own, both analytically and empirically.

PREFACE

All the papers in this symposium take this inextricable involvement as their point of departure, and attempt to illustrate the different levels at which the interaction between pastoralists and non-pastoralists occurs. Some focus on the micro-level and some on the macro-level. Most of the papers are not concerned to elaborate a systematic theoretical framework for the study of nomad-sedentary relations in general. A few attempts have been made in this direction, and although these have considerable intrinsic interest, it must be admitted that they were met with some degree of skepticism at the symposium. Taken together, the papers present a relatively broad range of empirical data which provides us with an enlightening picture of some of the ways in which a culturally recognized and ecologically specialized category of people fit into the general fabric of Middle Eastern life. As such they are offered as a contribution to anthropological literature on both pastoral nomadic societies and Middle Eastern cultures.

As editor of this volume I would like to express my deepest appreciation to the Institute of International Studies, University of California, Berkeley, for giving me the opportunity to spend part of my sabbatical year as a Visiting Research Associate at the Institute working on this volume. Specifically, I would like to thank Professors Ernst B. Haas and Neil J. Smelser, Directors of the Institute, for their enthusiasm in encouraging me to prepare these papers for publication in the Institute's monograph series, and to Paul Gilchrist for his invaluable editing assistance.

Cynthia Nelson

Berkeley, California
August 1973

CONTENTS

NOTES ON CONTRIBUTORS

CYNTHIA NELSON is Professor of Anthropology at The American University in Cairo.

TALAL ASAD is Associate Professor of Social Anthropology at the University of Hull, England.

FREDRIK BARTH is Professor of Social Anthropology at the University of Bergen, Norway.

ABADALLA SAID BUJRA is Associate Professor of Social Anthropology and Acting Head, Department of Sociology, University of Dar es Salaam, Tanzania.

DONALD P. COLE is Visiting Assistant Professor of Anthropology at the University of California, Berkeley.

G. REZA FAZEL is Assistant Professor of Anthropology at the University of Massachusetts at Boston.

ERNEST GELLNER is Professor of Philosophy at the London School of Economics and Political Science.

ABDEL GHAFFAR M. AHMED is Lecturer in Anthropology at the University of Khartoum, Sudan.

ABBAS MOHAMMED is Lecturer in Anthropology at the University of Khartoum, Sudan.

G.J. OBERMEYER is Assistant Professor of Anthropology at the American University in Beirut, Lebanon.

W.W. SWIDLER is Associate Professor of Anthropology at the Liberal Arts College, Fordham University (New York).

INTRODUCTION:
APPROACHES TO NOMADISM

Many of the papers in this symposium represent an attempt to develop a new conceptualization of nomadism. As such, they are expressions of optimism--perhaps justified. Conceptualizations, at least those which are both good and new, do not come to order, even at the behest of a highly successful, informative, and illuminating collection of papers such as the present one. New conceptualizations cannot be ordered, and their crystallization is a mysterious process. But what one can do--and what I shall attempt to do--is to schematize the material to some extent, and comment on the problems which arise in its ordering and interpretation.

First of all, some negative points concerning omissions. Is one to discuss nomadism as such, or nomadism in the Middle East? The general title refers to nomadism as such, yet the extraordinarily valuable concrete material is specifically Middle Eastern. Obviously one could use the material either way. One could use it either to check generalizations about nomadism as such--i.e., nomadism anywhere; or, alternatively, one could restrict oneself to using it to try to elaborate a theory of nomadism in a particular cultural context--namely, that of the Middle East. Either exercise would be valuable, and there is I suppose no reason whatsoever why both should not be attempted together. But they must be distinguished. The problems of comparative method which are involved are quite different, according to which one of the two questions one attempts to tackle.

The material is not of course altogether limited to Middle Eastern situations. As one might expect from a gathering amongst which social anthropologists predominate, there are allusions to nomadic situations in sub-Saharan Africa. But there is not a great deal else. To be specific, the name of Owen Lattimore is conspicuous by its absence.

Yet surely this is a most remarkable, promising, and curiously unexploited area for comparative investigation. The history of the Islamic Middle East can, from its very beginnings, be written to a large extent in terms of the interaction between the nomads and the sedentary and urban populations. The same approach can also be made central--and has by some writers been made central--in the study of those Far Eastern cultures which include both nomadic populations and centralized societies based on irrigation agriculture in river valleys. Both the similarities and the contrasts are conspicuous. Does this not deserve very thorough exploration as part of any attempt to understand the role of nomadism in general?

A second very general comparative question which, it seems to me, has to be faced arises from quite a different contrast--not the contrast between two great, complex civilizations, each of which includes nomads as an important factor in its political and economic balance, but the contrast between any complex civilization which includes nomads and, on the other hand, nomads who are (so to speak) on their own. One could formulate this distinction in terms of the difference between symbiotic nomadism and simple nomadism. Middle Eastern nomadism is, I believe, invariably symbiotic. In fact, it is reasonable to suppose that many of the pervasive cultural traits of the region are built around and facilitate this symbiosis. This specificity and both what separates it from and what it shares with simple or primitive nomadism deserve full exploration.

Once one begins to look specifically at symbiotic nomadism, and even more specifically at Middle Eastern symbiotic nomadism, one needs to look not merely at one but at all the partners in the relationship. There is reason to assume that there are more than two. In the Middle East it appears that, at the very least, three partners are involved--nomads, sedentarized peasants, and urban populations. One needs to look above all at the curious stability or permanence of the relationship in the Middle East. Nomads have existed elsewhere, but have seldom remained quite so permanent a feature on the scene. For instance, there is a well-known historical theory which involves the Magyar nomads as an important factor in the emergence of European feudalism, but it is noteworthy that they did not remain nomads. In southeast Europe, nomadism was on the retreat long before anything comparable happened in the Middle East.

The understanding of this relatively stable symbiotic relationship ought to result in providing for it something like that which Wittfogel provides for Oriental despotism--a basic, easily intelligible and manipulable model which, whether or not we accept it in the end, serves as a useful starting point or baseline for a theoretical understanding of the total social structure.[1] Wittfogel's model, so fashionable in recent decades, is most conspicuously inadequate for the typical Muslim state, which approximates it only in the representations of its political theorists, not in its political realities. The ruler may claim absolute power, but he seldom possesses it. Even less often does he have at his command a genuine, efficient, and obedient bureaucracy. The central state is, as modern liberals would wish it (though not at all in the sense in which they would wish it), but one agency amongst others in the society, which has to temporize, negotiate, balance, play-off, and so forth. The claims that have been made for Wittfogel's model for the Middle East and the Muslim world seem to me totally unjustified, whatever their merit may be for regions further east. Robert Fernea's recent book on southern Iraq gives a striking demonstration of the inadequacy of that model, not merely for regions where one might expect it to be inapplicable, such as mountainous and desert areas, but also for a region where one would expect it to apply--namely, the almost paradigmatically hydraulic area of southern Mesopotamia.[2] He casts doubt on the theory, widely accepted both by members of the culture and its external students, of the destruction of the irrigation system by Hulagu, and contends that the system continued and was apparently much better run by a highly decentralized tribal organization than by the subsequently superimposed Turkish and British bureaucracies.

The remarkable success of southern Iraqui tribesmen, with their segmentary organization, in running a hydraulic system brings to mind an issue which, it seems to me, deserves more systematic treatment--namely, the applicability of the segmentary model of internal tribal organization. This idea, whose ancestor is Durkheim and which in its modern form was developed by Evans-Pritchard, is highly relevant to this symposium. In recent years, its history has been curious. Originally the property of social anthropologists, its recent successes have tended to be outside anthropology, where it has been extensively borrowed, but used in a very loose manner, by political scientists and others. Within anthropology itself, there has been a tendency to see it merely as a model--an image of social organization which is present in the minds of the participants, but which is honored more in the breach than in the observance. People talk about segmentation, it is said, but they do not "practice" it.

I am by no means convinced of the justice of this downgrading of the notion of segmentation, most particularly when we deal with Middle Eastern material. Various things can be said in defense of the segmentation theory.

Those who insist that it is merely a model--the way people think, and not the way they act and organize their social relationships--are liable to confuse a number of issues. It is of course true that the typical segmentary image of the genesis of a tribal society as a fanning out of descendants from a single apical point is not accurate. This by itself, however, does not preclude the spurious or simplified genealogy from being a good approximation of political behavior, of the way in which groups are in conflict but nevertheless unite against larger enemies, and so forth. Here there is the danger that the critics are rejecting a position which deserves to be maintained. If the segmentary structure is conceived as absolutely rigid, as inescapably predetermining the alignments of individuals and groups in all conflicts, then of course it is invalid. The only claims which I think ought to be attributed to the model are the following: (1) the opposition of various groups, at each level of size, is the main agency for maintaining order, and (2) in the maintenance of order and in defining the groups that balance each other the most important, but not the only, criterion is coextension with the kin and territorial definitions which operate within the society itself. A society which satisfies these conditions can most usefully be classified as segmentary, and we deprive ourselves of very valuable analysis if we discard the segmentary model as simply an image, not a reality. I am firmly convinced that societies exist, notably in the Middle East, which do or did satisfy these conditions.

There is moreover a very specific point at which the notion of segmentation is invaluable. Segmentation is intimately connected with a certain kind of equality, specifically the equality of power and of the ability to impose sanctions on others. In segmentary societies power is evenly diffused, to a very unusual degree, over the whole social structure. This is sometimes denied but, in my view, erroneously. (There are societies in which power is evenly diffused which have tree-like genealogies, or systems of conceiving groups and locations of individuals within them, but the principle by which order is maintained within them is then not segmentary.) The theory of the mechanics of a segmentary society hinges on the fact that there is no center at which the means of cohesion are concentrated and which can impose its will on other groups. Everybody has to combine, in the approved segmentary manner, for purposes of self-defense and the deterrence of aggression. Such equality is of course only an approximation, but segmentary societies come much closer to equality of power than do most others.

In a sense, the theory of segmentation is a kind of inversion of Hobbes. Hobbes believed that because men are equal, roughly speaking, in the amount of harm they can do each other, they have to establish a centralized state, an absolute sovereign. If they are unequal, it is in the interest of those who are privileged, in terms of the power to coerce, not to submit to a central sovereign. In fact, the opposite appears to be true. In conditions in which men are roughly equal, it appears to be _less_ feasible to erect a central state than to erect a viable system which is uncentralized, "stateless." On the other hand, once technology or geography puts some individual or group in a commanding position, it is possible to establish a powerful state.

The relevance of all this to the Middle Eastern situation is considerable. The most conspicuous change in the Middle East in the past century or so is the tilting of the balance of power away from dissident tribal societies in favor of the central state. The means of coercion are far more unevenly distributed than they were before. Military, administrative, and communication technology is such as to make central enforcement far more effective. The social consequences of this are of course by no means limited to the strengthening of the power of the central authorities in the literal and narrow sense. An important consequence of the change is that power is also conferred on those who possess, or are believed to possess, means of access to and influence with the central authorities. In other words, a patronage network tends to replace thé traditional segmentary structure. However, the segmentary ideology or image of society--in particular the patrilineal vision, which is a specific variant of it--persists, and continues to color the way in which people think and talk. It is here that the danger arises of depriving ourselves of a valuable tool. If we insist that the segmentary picture was always and inherently an image and not a reality, we have no way of saying something which, to my mind, is conspicuously true--namely, that though segmentation is indeed largely an image in contemporary, well-centralized situations, it was very much of a reality in previous decentralized conditions. Something which is intrinsically an illusion can hardly have become <u>more</u> of an illusion now. If all segmentary self-images are delusory, it is hard to say that some are more so than others. But in fact it seems most obvious to me that some are indeed more delusory than others. We must retain a way of characterizing the recent general change from segmentation to patronage.

An unselective, indiscriminate condemnation of all segmentary ideology as <u>mere ideology</u> prevents us from either noting or seeing this. This important point can be made without prejudice to the question of the extent to which the segmentary picture is indeed a reality. I believe it to be such to quite a considerable extent, in many important cases, without believing that the segmentary principle ever completely explains the maintenance of order in any society, or believing that it should ever be taken entirely at face value in the way in which it is conceived from the inside by participants.

It may be worth stating why it is so much of a reality in certain cases. The most important evidence for this seems to me indirect. It is drawn from situations in which very complex tasks are carried out over extensive territories by large numbers of people without anything much in the way of formal, hierarchical organization or authority and enforcement. When tribesmen without strong or permanent leaders with means of coercion at their disposal nevertheless combine and maintain an irrigation network, or cooperate in the maintenance and careful husbandry of pastures, then some kind of principle of coercion and organization must be at work. If the leadership is weak and the means of coercion and sanctions at its disposal are minimal, then that principle cannot be specialized political leadership with centralized power and enforcement. What then is it? If the societies in question have a segmentary ideology and a segmentary system of defining groups and subgroups, and those groups are clearly identifiable on that ground and are seen to cooperate and to oppose each other in roughly the way the segmentary model requires, then until someone comes up with a better explanation, we are justified in concluding that the segmentary system is a reality as well as an image. If at some later date, the superimposition of a newly powerful state completely redistributes power, one can then say that the segmentary idea has become an illusion. But it is an illustion *in contrast with a previous reality*, rather than inherently and always a myth.

This error of viewing the segmentary model as an image only, if such it be, comes most naturally to anthropologists who study a Middle Eastern society at a late, contemporary stage of development, and who combine an interest in the past with a disinclination to believe that it was discontinuous with the present. In this they tend to receive encouragement from the current political/intellectual climate. The contemporary state is not inclined to encourage tribal dissidence by reminding tribesmen of their past habits, and unlike colonial administrations, it is unlikely to romanticize tribes--at any rate when it is in direct contact with them. An anthropologist who receives his informants in a villa in a town will note that they *talk* segmentation but fail to practice it; they *act* patronage. In an urban and semi-modern context within a modern state, it would be most surprising if this were not the case. But it is rash for him to assume that things were always so. Even today, if one looks at the collective ownership of pasture and the way in which its use is sanctioned, one can get the feel of the reality of segmentary organization.

So much for some of the general considerations which arise in the study of Middle Eastern nomadism--or nomadism in general. I shall now look specifically at what the contributors to the present symposium have done. In their theoretical approach to their subject, many or all of them have attempted a kind of accountancy, a kind of "balance-of-payments" approach, which tries to work out how various services or benefits flow and are balanced. This approach is widely shared among anthropologists. Within this approach one can distinguish two grand moieties, two great segments. Which segment one belongs to depends on whether one concentrates on the flow of *goods* or on the balance of *power*. The two approaches share something which I think generally characterizes the structural approach in anthropology--i.e., there is an attempt to show how, given the interests of the participants and the distribution of resources amongst them, they are constrained by the resulting situation into courses of action which result in the kind of situation which is observed.

Within this general approach, a good deal depends on whether one feels that the crux is economic or political, whether one is concerned primarily with the means of production or the means of coercion. Perhaps there is also a third and intermediate group--those who concentrate on the institutions of mediation between nomads and others. I shall refrain from assigning individual contributors to any of these groups. Let their material speak for itself.

In a very, very loose sense, as a kind of shorthand, one could refer to those who believe the means of production to be fundamental as the "Marxists." It is ironic that this kind of very general Marxism, in the sense of concentration on the means of production and the resulting ecological equilibrium, does not seem to result either from the influence of Marx himself or from characteristically Marxist concerns. Apart from its origin in certain recent theoretical developments such as exchange theory, it seems on the contrary to spring from a kind of overconcentration on the present, with a possibly unwitting assumption that the past resembled it, and from a failure to be sufficiently concerned with the political specificity of the present. This specificity of the present is the same as that which I stressed in connection with the discussion of segmentation: it is the outstanding power of the modern state. This may mislead one in taking the maintenance of order for granted. When the state is so powerful that it succeeds in approximating to the Weberian definition and monopolizing legitimate coercion, then it follows that nomadism becomes an economic rather than a political adaptation--the solution of an economic rather than a political problem.

The political order has been preempted. But it does not seem to me at all obvious that it was always so. Of course, nomads have always had to eat in order to live, and nomadism has always been a solution to an economic problem, but it is not clear to me that, in the past, its institutions were molded more by economic than by political considerations. Perhaps they were. This is a central question for investigation rather than one to be prejudged by looking too exclusively at contemporary situations, in which many nomads have been prevented from offering solutions to political problems through not having enough political power. Our "Marxists"--or should one say "economically oriented anthropologists?"--are in danger of falling into what might be called the "laissez-faire illusion" of taking the political order for granted. An anthropologists should never do that. The political center may be out of the reach of the nomad nowadays, relatively speaking, but this is not part of the nature of things. It is a particular socail condition which requires examination.

As for the past, one should at least look at the possibility that it was the distribution and the application of the means of coercion, rather than the means of production, which was most crucial. It is noteworthy that in one of the papers which is firmly oriented toward the past, Dr. Asad's charming historical vignettes--presumably because they look frankly at the past--are free of any tendency to ignore the political realm.

The intermediate group of papers, which look at mediation and brokerage with the central society, of course do not ignore the political, though they are concerned with a form of politics which is characteristic of a period when the central state is gaining in power, when it looks for channels of communication with the larger group which incorporates the nomads who--for their part--seek ways of influencing or approaching the central state and the ultimate holders of power within it.

Having made this plea for the importance of the political, and also for a sense of the time-bound validity of observations about the political realm, I would complement it with a plea for another kind of accountancy which is relatively lacking in the papers in this symposium: the religious. There is of course a well-known group of problems in religious sociology concerning nomads: Are they conspicuously devoid of religious ritual? If so, why? Are they notorious for religious laxity, but at the same time available for enlistment in fanatical puritanical religious movements for which they supply the sword arm and from which they borrow legitimation for pillage? These are stereotypes--but not necessarily invalid because they are such. The unity of Middle Eastern civilization is notoriously a religious one, and its particular institutions may well have been formed to a significant extent by the need to provide mediation and brokerage through religion in the various past forms of the balance between nomads and non-nomads. This issue deserves a much fuller exploration, as does the position of women--a theme discussed by Dr. Nelson which has intimate connections with religion.

These, then, are the topics which will have to be considered in a general theory of nomadism. Nomadism is not the same in various civilizations, and can occur either as part of a wider equilibrium or in small self-contained communities. The nomadic unit has an internal structure, and so has the wider host society in those cases in which there is a wider framework. Apart from the internal structure of the tribe and the external relations to the state and/or non-nomadic society, there is the intriguing matter of the relationships between various tribal societies, all of them nomadic, though probably to varying degrees. For instance, in the Sahara belt stretching from the western desert of Egypt to Mauritania, there is a tendency to conceive of these relationships as stratified, and to attribute ranked specialization to specific tribes--the sword or the Book. This specialization and raking is often notional rather than real, and covers over a more subtle and complex reality. Both ideology and reality deserve further exploration.

The internal and external structures of the nomad groups (so to speak) can overlap at many points, and clearly overlap with the problem of brokerage both in the traditional and in the modern setting. Nomadism is an answer to both economic and political pressures, and the weight of these diverse pressures is subject to change. The present symposium has provided us with an admirable starting point for systematically analyzing these issues.

Ernest Gellner

Footnotes

[1]Karl A. Wittfogel, Oriental Despotism: A Comparative Study of Total Power (New Haven: Yale University Press, 1957).

[2]Robert Fernea, Shaykh and Effendi: Changing Patterns of Authority among the El Shabana of Southern Iraq (Harvard Middle Eastern Studies Series, No. 14, 1970).

A GENERAL PERSPECTIVE ON NOMAD-SEDENTARY RELATIONS IN THE MIDDLE EAST

Fredrik Barth

General Argument

To analyze nomad-sedentary relations we need a model that exhibits the crucial features of these relations, so that we can compare their variations under a unified perspective. Various alternatives present themselves: (1) We can depict nomadic society in its relation to its total environment. Sedentary peoples and societies are part of this total environment, and the nomads' relations to them are revealed as part of an ecologic, economic, or political analysis. (I have adopted this general viewpoint in my analysis of the Basseri of South Persia.)[1] (2) We can take a more explicitly symbiotic view, and seek to analyze the interconnections of nomads and sedentary as prerequisites for the persistence of each in their present form. (The paper by Abdel Ghaffar in the present collection may serve to exemplify some advantages of this view, and the insight it sheds on the joint system in which both nomads and settled populations participate.)

Both these perspectives are problematical for comparative work because the features they bring out are specific to particular cases, and the general framework provides only an opportunity to identify similarities and differences. How does this help us to understand the sources from which such similarities and differences derive? To make analytical comparisons, we need to identify some crucial variables and observe their impact on the system as a whole. Thus we should develop a model whereby we can characterize the difference between nomads and settled along some common dimensions, and then seek to discover how variations in the characteristics of either group along these dimensions affect the larger system of which they are part. In most cases, the contrast between nomad and settled rests both on their distinctive territorial patterns--shifting vs. sedentary--and on their distinctive subsistence patterns--pastoral vs. agricultural. (The aberrant cases--nomadic non-pastoralists, like gypsies, or sedentary non-agriculturalists, like fishermen--need not concern us now, but may become crucial test cases later.) The two characteristics are clearly functionally connected; yet they may be quite independent in their analytical consequences.

Let me suggest that it is perhaps not the distinction nomadic or movable vs. settled that provides the vital focus for understanding the relations between the two groups but rather the differences in their systems of production, in terms of which they adapt and exchange and articulate. Let us therefore provisionally focus on the differing character of pastoral and agricultural activities. (3) We can focus not on two kinds of society, but--initially--on the total activities of a region. If we stop for a while thinking basically of groups of people, and think instead of types of activity, we can then disaggregate the activities that take place in a region into some middle-range sub-systems which are systems of production, or "productive regimes."[2] In the traditional Middle East we will see respectively pastoralism, agriculture, crafts, trade, etc. Coon has made us aware of how these often seem to define community types;[3] let us first look at them rather as separate, internally organized activity systems, somewhat in the manner in which the economist speaks of "sectors" of the economy. This will ultimately bring both nomads and settled populations in a region under a common perspective, whereby we can see how they relate to each other in terms of dependence, dominance, and stratification. Having analyzed their characteristics, we may then be able to understand the dynamics of each such sub-system or regime. Only then do I propose that we look at the overall social organization that ties one or several such regimes to a persisting social unit and a community type. We can then ask what the dynamic implications are for those communities of the productive regimes under which they exist, and we can analyze the interconnections of the communities of the region in terms of these dynamics.

In developing the present argument, I am working on the hypothesis that the pastoral regime of production has essential properties which contrast with the other productive regimes of a region, and which in various modulations determine the form and relations of nomads, dependent on this regime for their maintenance, to the other population sectors of the region.

The basic argument of this paper is thus built in strata which, it is hoped, become increasingly empirically adequate as we go along. I am simply trying to set up the dimensions for comparison, and sort out their implications step-by-step.

Basic Characteristics of the Productive Regimes

To develop this argument, I shall first focus on the pastoral regime in terms of the nature of pastoral capital, and the options it provides for the person or group that makes management decisions.[4] The notable features are (a) that saving and investment are necessary under all circumstances--the herd capital is perishable and must be replaced--and (b) such investment is possible without benefit of any economic institutions, since one of the main products of the herd is lambs/calves, etc.

Contrast this with the conditions of production in an agricultural regime where (a) land is essentially imperishable and cannot be consumed by the management unit except by benefit of elaborate economic institutions that facilitate its conversion to food, and (b) land cannot be increased by investment of its product (crops) except where economic institutions exist to effect its conversion.*

The consequences of these basic differences in productive regime are striking, particularly with respect to the growth potential of the units of enterprise that engage in them. Expansion of the enterprise must depend on increased investment in one or several production factors (including technical innovation). Enterprise in the pastoral sector is always faced with the possibility of rapid growth (or decline) regardless of what the public economic institutions and facilities may be, because part of its product comes automatically in the form of capital gains, which only an active management decision to slaughter will remove from reinvestment. Enterprise in the agricultural sector, on the other hand, has no such ready way of growth; unless special institutional public facilities for conversion exist, it will stagnate from lack of investment opportunities. Obviously, different agricultural societies have developed different institutional facilities which serve with varying success to increase investment and growth in agricultural enterprises. These institutional complexes may take the form of Feasts of Merit, in which food is converted to rank. They may make possible the conversion food ⟶ warriors ⟶ land by conquest in anarchic feasting societies. They may allow for the conversion food ⟶ labor ⟶ land, for example, in slave societies with low population density, or crops ⟶ exchange media ⟶ capital goods and land in elaborate market systems. Of special interest in the Middle East is

---

*It might be argued that the differences are not especially great, since both productive regimes require the same basic kinds of production factors: (1) land (= pastures) + capital (= herds) + labor, or (2) land (= fields) + capital (= seed) + labor, and the capital factor is equally perishable and replaceable in both. Two immutable differences between the two regimes must, however, be remembered: the rate of return on seed is high (ten-fifty-fold in Middle East cereal crops), so its value is low and attainability simple, while the rate of return on flocks rarely reaches onefold, so the capital value is high and availability by loan, etc., problematical. In its foundations, agriculture is therefore labor-intensive, while pastoralism is capital-intensive. On the other hand, the time required to extract value from land is great in agriculture, so control of land is essential, while the time required by grazing is minimal, so control may well be precarious and ad hoc.

capitalization and intensification of agriculture by the conversion food ⟶ labor ⟶ irrigation investment ⟶ new or increasingly productive land. The existence of either or several of these complexes will in a direct way modify the properties of capital in the agricultural sector by modifying the options open to management. They will thus affect the dynamic potential of agricultural activity, so the picture will rarely be that of an unmodified pastoral buoyancy and agricultural stagnation. But in any real-life situation, one would expect some trace of the contrast to remain between a pastoral potential independent of any collective economic institutions and an agricultural sector dependent on the proper functioning of such institutions and hampered and canalized by their specific forms. To understand the balance between these two sectors in a particular situation, we thus need to note the particular properties of these institutional facilities.

Relation of Household Units to the Major Regimes

We have focused so far on the activity system of each regime and the enterprise that may be based on each. But to what extent such activity systems are organized as specialized socioeconomic enterprises is an entirely open question of social organization. In most societies they are not, and the activities are pursued by multi-purpose households, often involved in the activities of several regimes simultaneously.

Some Middle Eastern nomads are, as we know, organized in households wholly or predominantly basing their livelihood on the pastoral regime. It should follow from the preceding argument that groups of such households will always have the potentiality of economic take-off: in prosperous times their enterprise will expand, their capital will increase, their economy will grow. Compare this to the classical peasant situation as described from many parts of the world: households are tied to an agricultural regime with blockage against reinvestment and growth, with a fraction of the product constantly tapped off by a tax or rent system, and with population growth and household subdivision dissipating whatever small surpluses may temporarily appear.[5]

On the other hand, many households practice a mixed economy based on a combination of agricultural and pastoral regimes. We need materials to analyze the transfers of capital and product between these two sectors of the household economy achieved by adjusting consumption and allocating labor internally in the household. The variety of such adaptations in the Middle East should not be underestimated. In some cases they are readily recognizable in various forms of seasonal transhumance; in most cases we may expect long-term pulsations, with groups shifting between a pastoral and an agricultural role. (Warren

Swidler's contribution to this volume provides some material on these topics.)

So far, I have argued only in terms of management options, and not considered the social characteristics and wider contexts of the persons or groups who constitute the management units, and how these affect the decisions made and policies pursued. To understand the position of households with mixed economies, as compared to those tied closely to only one type of regime, it is useful to anticipate this broader discussion somewhat. Growth does not result from the existence of an investment option, but from actors' choosing that option. In the case of households based entirely on pastoralism, I have described elsewhere the way the operation of such enterprises leads frequently to a compulsive husbandry of capital, saving, and investment.[6] Essentially, because of the insecurity of the capital and the expenditure of labor being directed predominantly to capital maintenance, there is no cut-out of productive effort when a threshold of results is reached--a nomad's day never ends. One can see the signs of this very widely among nomads, from the "overstocking" of African pastoral areas to the relentless flock-building of reindeer nomads.

In the case of households with mixed economies, on the other hand, I would guess that "the Sahlins effect"[7] of the domestic mode of production frequently makes itself felt. The buoyancy of the pastoral sector in their economy may make such mixed-economy farmers more prosperous than their more purely agricultural fellows, even if they tend to occupy much more marginal areas; however, left to their own devices, they do not pursue growth relentlessly, but are happy to remain small farmers once a certain level is reached. When is this so; what kind of organizational superstructures might weld mixed farmers together, or exploit them, for expansive purposes; and when do they themselves, despite a domestic organization of production, choose to maximize capital growth? These become crucial (and so far unanswered) questions in the kind of comparative perspective outlined here.

We also need to consider the administrative and technical circumstances under which irrigation enterprises prosper and grow. The present intensification of irrigation agriculture in the Middle East is not entirely unprecedented, and we need to consider what have been the bases for similar sectorial take-offs in previous times. Indeed, it may be a characteristic of the agricultural sector that, during phases of technological change or smooth administrative and institutional functioning, it is characterized by growth periods that in their aggregate size and implications are quite breathtaking as compared to events in the nomadic sector.

Finally, any analysis of the balance between peoples of the pasture and peoples of the sown must take account of the other, often subsidiary, regimes of trade and transport, crafts, and warfare--the last involving military technology, geography, and mobilizable population mass. In this provisional discussion, however, I shall simplify the model to concentrate essentially on the two major sectors of pastoralism and agriculture only.

Macro-Organization: The Connection Between Groups or Entities and Their Supporting Regimes

From first principles it is apparent that social macro-entities such as ethnic groups, communities, tribes, or classes have no necessary one-to-one relation to pastoral or agricultural regimes of production. The divisions between such entities may or may not coincide with the lines of distinction between these regimes. Thus pastoralist may be merely an occupational category, as is trader or craftsman in many societies, or it may be descriptive of whole tribes or peoples. What are the conditions under which a social entity in a region has a special linkage with a particular type of productive regime, and what are the dynamic consequences of such linkage on the persistence and/or change of the entity or group? Essentially, I am proposing that the relations and dynamics of such groups may derive from what may be described as their mode of production* within a larger regional economy.

Let me illustrate the point with a generalized, relatively categorical example. If we compare most East African Nilotic and Nilo-Hamitic societies with societies previously called Hamitic kingdoms (e.g., Rwanda, Burundi), we will find in both regional economies without market facilities for transforming capital, and containing agricultural and pastoral sectors. Where both these kinds of activity are pursued by households with mixed economies, as among the Nuer, Karamajong, etc., we generally find egalitarian, homogeneous societies. Where each sector is monopolized by a discrete ethnic group, I would argue that it is well-nigh automatic and inevitable that the pastoral group, favored by the inherent potential of the pastoral regime of production, will have the advantage over the agriculturalists, and by virtue of their mode of production become the dominant group. This dominance of the pastoral group within kingdoms is of course well-established in the descriptive literature concerning East Africa. What inequality we see is not the instituted effect of past acts of conquest, but the continuing effect of the inherent growth potential of pastoral production tied to a self-perpetuating

---

*I use this expression in what I take to be the usual sense--i.e., an economic regime plus its associated context of social organization.

group.[8] If the social organization is such as to allow occupational specialization, but no ethnic division, a class division should emerge inevitably, favoring the controllers of pastoral capital. Only social institutions effectively preventing such specialization, or directly counteracting the growth potential of pastoral capital, could prevent the development of gross social differences.

What I am proposing, then, so as to bring nomadic and sedentary populations into a common analytic framework and understand the forms and variations in the relationships between them is (a) to look at them as participants in a common regional economy, (b) to understand the character of the productive regimes that each is associated with, and (c) to analyze the class relationships between them. This we can do without wedding ourselves to any preconceived schemata, but simply by inquiring systematically into the facts in each case. I would expect us to find, in varying degrees, depending on the factors noted above which affect the balance between the pastoral and agricultural sectors, that the growth capacity of the pastoral enterprises gives them an advantage over the agricultural enterprises, so that there is a tendency for an income flow to be set up from the agricultural to the pastoral sector. This is not the whole story, but let us stop there for a moment. _If_ such an income flow is set up, it would lead, by steps that it should not be necessary to spell out, to an accumulation of wealth and influence in the hands of the pastoralists, and to a system of stratification in which they predominate.

The situation in the Middle East, however, is far more complex and variable than this, for two main reasons. Not only do market and other economic facilities exist that allow various types of reinvestment in the agricultural sector, and thus a highly variable balance of advantage between the two sectors, but also pastoralists are related to the peoples of the sown in other ways than through the food market--i.e., they are their customers for specialized services and luxury goods, they participate in their religion and high culture, they aspire to their wealth, power, and status. Moreover, all is not just domestic economy and markets: there is an ever-present taxing state structure which initiates and controls production and trade, at least in some kinds of goods. The regional picture of growth within sectors and flows of surpluses between sectors can thus only be depicted by a detailed analysis of the interplay of a variety of factors, but nonetheless it may derive its main dynamism from the two contrasting modes of production.

The basic pattern in the Middle East might be sketched as follows: On the domestic level, within local areas, an income flow tends to be set up from agricultural units to pastoral units, sustaining a local dominance by the pastoralists. However, cities with their urban elites, controlling the state apparatus, also prey on the cultivating households, and they do so by very effective and stable force and control, making peasants of the cultivators and drawing a substantial tax flow from them. Through this there is a tendency for the peasant households to be ground down even further by debt burdens to middleman entrepreneurs.

These state systems, however, have great difficulties controlling and dominating nomadic pastoralists, who may choose among several strategies in their accommodation to the state: submitting to it in return for peace, withdrawing and defending themselves from it to avoid the tax drain, or seeking control by attempting conquest of the whole state apparatus. But any rising local elite of pastoralists, no matter what policy they choose vis-à-vis the state, tends to be drawn into the wider system of stratification obtaining in the region as a whole, and therefore to embroil themselves in competition with urban elites--perhaps reversing income flows and dissipating advantages that have been won.

Thus we might be able to account for the seesaw of power between nomad confederacies and irrigation states, and the expansion and contraction of city bureaucracies vis-à-vis tribal marches and freelands that have characterized most Middle Eastern regions by such an analysis. But to do so, we would need to reorganize and probably supplement the available materials on social and cultural variation in the area.

Some Questions from the Middle Eastern Material

The universal integration in the Middle East of the pastoral and agricultural sectors of production into one regional economy is evidenced by the basic similarity of the diet consumed in tents and in villages, which is composed of both agricultural and pastoral products.[9] In this respect the nomads of the Middle East seem to be similar to the nomads of most areas, though some East African cattle people and some North Asian herders may be exceptions. As for the growth capacity of the pastoral enterprise, this will surely vary according to ecologic circumstances, but can safely be assumed, at least for long periods, to be positive. Given these two circumstances, we would expect to find long-term trends in exchange relations and capital accumulation that favor the more pastorally oriented sector of the population, and particularly full-fledged pastoral nomads, leading to the dominance of such groups in local systems of stratification.

Such indeed has been the case at various times and in a great number of local situations. Characteristically, if one analyzes the elites in small towns, villages, and the countryside in the traditional Middle East, it is nomads--and traders--who have been actively upwardly mobile, while cultivators form the stable bottom of the pyramid, and landowners (in part) occupy the top positions, but are sustained there by stagnated enterprises. However, we must take into account a third circumstance: the existence of state structures with a sedentary base. These state structures pursue strategies that interfere with the "free play" of economic processes. States have a "nomad policy," whereas nomads, since the days of the Mongols, can hardly be said to have an "agrarian policy"; they merely benefit from the buoyancy of their aggregate household economies. This lack of a long-term policy means that nomadic success and growth will need to be followed by diversification if the nomads are to have any hope of long-term political success. Pastoral growth and dominance, unless checked by other factors, will sooner or later evoke state countermeasures designed to contain, exploit, or destroy pastoral nomad ascendancy. The centripetal conquest of the state apparatus by a particular nomad tribe, as frequently seen in Persian history for example, would not change this, since the formerly nomadic dynasty would have the same interests as the previous controllers of the sedentary state--at least vis-à-vis all tribes but their own.

The balance between the pasture and the sown, as found in any particular region of the Middle East, should thus be understandable in terms of the following basic factors:

(1) The local possibilities for profit conversion to investment and growth in the agricultural sector of the economy, producing a local sedentary elite with specific interests and capacities. This will affect the nature and magnitude of the pastoralists' advantage, but for most places and times leave them dominant. The extent of dominance by the pastoralists will then depend on

(2) Negative feedback relating to the growth of influence by the pastoral sector of the population:

(a) Ecologic controls: Herd losses and other disasters leading to collapse of established control, or population growth leading to over-pressure and impoverishment;[10]

(b) Internal stratification: Processes whereby wealth above a certain threshold is dissipated within the pastoral sector through feasting, warfare, and other elite consumption;

(c) Regional stratification: Processes whereby wealth, often in support of elite personnel, flows from the pastoral sector to the sedentary centers to sustain claims to rank in the larger cosmopolitan state;

(d) State countermeasures: Actions to contain a local pastoral elite, to exploit it, to drain its wealth, or to eliminate the group when the costs of controlling it are too high.

Some of these factors may be illustrated with material from various Iranian-speaking groups. In this south central Asian area, the last-resort attempts by states to put down nomads are familiar, tempered in Afghanistan by the ethnic association of most nomads with the precariously dominant group in a plural society.[11]

Looking at the southern chain of peoples--various Kurds, Lur, Bakhtiari, Boir Ahmed, Qashqai, Khamseh, various Baluch, the Ghilzai-Powindah cluster--it is apparent that in many regions we find a fusion of pure pastoralists and mixed farmers in part-nomadic tribal units. Only some few Kurds (Hakkari, Jaf), the Khamseh, and the Powindah stand out as fully pastoral nomadic tribes. The rest seem to exemplify the situation where a locally dominant pastoral sector is controlled mainly by factor (b) above--the dissipation of wealth as an effect of internal stratification--though doubtless (as in the case of the Bakhtiari and Qashqai) competition for cosmopolitan rank also plays a part. Clearly, attention must be paid to the consolidation of mixed farmers into strong tribal polities, such as in parts of Kurdistan and among southern and central Pathans, where specialized pastoralists (Hakkari, Jaf, Powindah) seem to be in a position similar to that of the Basseri and other Khamseh--transients without local dominance.

There is a need for comparative material from other parts of the Middle East, particularly on the local vs. cosmopolitan question of pastoral dominance--e.g., Arabian bedouin, Touareg, etc.--and how these might be understood in terms of the negative feedback noted above. Also, the social correlates of the pastoral and the agricultural sectors in the economies of Cyrenaica and the Maghreb seem unclear.

I hope that the framework sketched here will provide illumination on some major historical puzzles, such as the virtual disappearance of pastoral nomads from India after a long period of apparent importance, or the insignificance of true pastoral nomads on the cultural history of Europe. At present, however, we are particularly in need of closely reasoned analyses of a variety of local nomad-sedentary systems to test hypotheses of the type advanced here. Though data for such analyses can still be gathered (and historical materials can be exploited), it should be noted that the modernization of a regional economy through full monetization of the factors of production, and the introduction of new investment alternatives in industrial enterprises, so changes the picture as to completely eliminate the patterns that have dominated the Middle East till now, and that have been the focus of this exploratory analysis.

Footnotes

[1]Fredrik Barth, Nomads of South Persia (Oslo, 1961).

[2]Karl Eric Knutsson, "Ploughland and Swidden: A Dual System of Agriculture in Western Ethiopia" (unpublished, 1970), and Clifford Geertz, Agricultural Involution: The Processes of Ecological Change in Indonesia (Berkeley, 1968).

[3]Carleton S. Coon, Caravan: The Story of the Middle East (London, 1951).

[4]Cf. Fredrik Barth, "Capital Investment and the Social Structure of a Pastoral Nomad Group in South Persia" in R. Firth and B.S. Yamey, eds., Capital, Saving and Credit in Peasant Societies (London, 1964).

[5]Eric Wolf, Peasants (Englewood Cliffs, 1966).

[6]Barth, Nomads of South Persia, and "Capital, Investment and the Social Structure . . . ."

[7]Marshall Sahlins, Stone Age Economics (Chicago, 1972).

[8]Cf. Jacques Maquet, "African Society: Sub-Saharan Africa" in International Encyclopedia of the Social Sciences (New York, 1968).

[9]See M.M. Arensberg, "A Comparative Analysis of Culture and Community: Peoples of the Old World" in C.M. Arensberg and S.T. Kimball, eds., Culture and Community (New York, 1965), and Fredrik Barth, "Nomadism in the Mountain and Plateau Areas of Southwest Asia" in The Problems of the Arid Zone (UNESCO, 1960).

[10]See the various mechanisms affecting population balance in Barth, Nomads of South Persia.

[11]K. Ferdinand, "Les Nomades afghans" in J. Humlum, ed., La Géographie de l'Afghanistan (Copenhagen, 1959).

ADAPTIVE PROCESSES REGULATING NOMAD-SEDENTARY INTERACTION IN THE MIDDLE EAST

W.W. Swidler

Pastoral nomadism may be seen as an adaptational system of one type of human community. All societies within the type, no matter how diverse the cultural elements, are confronted with common problems in exploiting the environment, for nomadism is a system of interaction between two or more animal species populations. The human use of other animals in a free-ranging environment, for subsistence and as capital, creates a type of ecosystem which we know little about and which needs further study.[1]

The discussion here will be restricted to various nomadic societies in the larger Middle East whose adaptations are to marginal environments, defined by unstable and shifting resources. We shall consider the kinds of constraints nomads face by virtue of their system requirements--that is, given animal stock as capital, we shall examine some of the principles of production in nomad economy and the ways they are adaptive to the exigencies of the nomadic environment.

Nomadic societies in the Middle East do not exist in isolated habitats. They are usually in contact with other nomads, with villages, markets, and towns. Furthermore, the data clearly indicate (contrary to the idealized view of nomadic peoples) that many nomads raise cereal crops, and are sometimes engaged in complex and demanding forms of cultivation and marketing. It is unrealistic to consider animal stock as the only form of capital or the only means through which nomadic peoples derive their livelihood, and as we look at nomadic societies in the Middle East it becomes clear that there is a close interplay between stock and grain, between grazing and cultivation, between the desert and the sown. Thus, one cannot ignore the roles of the agrarian village, market-towns, and cities in processes of nomad adaptation. (In a later part of this paper, we shall discuss the intricate balance of hills and plains resources among the Brahui of Baluchistan, and the seasonal alternation in the use of milk and grain products.)

Through the pioneering work of Fredrik Barth, Robert Pehrson, and Robert Paine, among others, we have come to know the nomadic condition as one in which there is a constant process of adjusting balances between three variables: available pastures, the animal population, and the human population.[2] As Barth has so lucidly demonstrated for the Basseri, nomadism is a precarious specialization, requiring the maintenance of both short-term and long-term ecologic balances.[3] But there has been little discussion of the role of other resources in nomad life, such as cultivation rights, access to revenue through land ownership, and cash funds through market sale. Little attention has been paid to the systematic transferability of animal stock to other forms of wealth such as land, wells, shops, and partnerships in various entrepreneurial endeavors--all of which presupposes contact with other kinds of communities.

Pastures and Pasturage[4]

Systems of deployment of animals over pastures and pasturage are functions of the nutrient and general health requirements of herd animals in specific environments. These requirements vary with the kinds of animals raised, the habitat (in terms of the quality and quantity of pasture), and the stock complex, where multiple herds require grazing strategies peculiar to each species. Nomads raising mixed sheep/goat herds alone face fewer pasture problems than do those with a full stock complex, composed of camels, sheep/goats, and cattle. The more fodder and stubble grazing available as a systematic feature of the economy, the less open pasture is necessary. In Baluchistan and southeastern Turkey, for example, the purchase of rights to stubble grazing on fallow fields is an integral part of the nomadic system, fulfilling pasturage requirements as well as providing villagers with necessary fertilizer.[5]

Variations in access to pastures are extreme and must be considered at two levels of organization: intra-group tenure and inter-group boundary maintenance. There is little detailed information in the literature on the ways in which nomadic populations maintain access to territories vis-à-vis other groups. In areas as diverse as Baluchistan, the Arabian peninsula, and the Sudan, tribal confederacies regularized tribal access to territories in the past by distributing land among component tribes or sections of tribes. Thus tribal "boundaries" were often nothing more than contiguous holdings of sections belonging to different tribes. Among the Basseri in Persia, where confederacy organization was weak, the tribes maintained traditional migration routes on a "time table" which gave specific tribes the right to follow certain routes (sing.: il-rah) at specific times and for a specified duration.[6] In Baluchistan, the Brahui confederacy was a military organization which was strongest during periods of territorial expansion. Tracts of land were given to individual tribes as blood-compensation (khon bahār) for supplying men-at-arms to the confederacy's fighting force (lashkar). An important factor in the development of the nomadic niche in Baluchistan was that the territory gained by the tribes was located in two distinct and contrasting ecologic zones, which provided the tribes continuous access to pastures throughout the year. At the present time, most tribal territories in the Middle East have been absorbed into the administrative divisions of national governments, which now regulate migration, expansion, raiding, and other forms of ecologic adjustment.

In contrast to the diversity in territory maintenance throughout the Middle East, the processes of territoriality--or intra-tribal tenure--are remarkably similar. Agnatic descent is the overriding principle of organization for granting access to pastures. The agnatic group, at various levels of genealogical inclusiveness, depending on the tribe, holds rights to grazing territories in varying degrees of exclusivity. Sometimes grazing territories are held weakly by traditional usufruct, as among the Brahui, some Bedouin, and the Tuareg (among whom, however, land is not held by agnatic sections), while in other populations such as the Basseri, oulad pastures are allotted by the chief, and access to pastures is highly stable and regularized. In other cases, as among the Kababish of the north-central Sudan, named clans do not possess rights to territorial resources or water, and even prior occupation gives no exclusive rights of usufruct.[7]

It is clear that some form of corporate access to pastures is the rule, and that individual ownership of pasture land would be intolerable under free-ranging conditions. In a system which requires unimpeded access to grazing territories, we would not expect rights of allocation and alienation to be held by individuals or family units. It would appear that in environments where there is little or no competition for grazing resources between separate tribes, territories are held by, or associated with, weakly bounded agnatic descent groups, where maneuverability in grazing choices is maximized. On the other hand, where tribal competition is strong for the same resources, as in the case of the Basseri, access to grazing areas is highly regularized, and the sanctions for infringement of rights are very specific. There appears to be little choice in this environment regarding migration routes, as we noted above.[8]

Animals

Several economic constraints are characteristic of nomadic systems. Some of the most obvious are: (1) the reproductive and productive capacities of the animals, and their effects on animal and human aggregations and dispersals, (2) the achievement of a minimum level of productive efficiency whereby management is geared to sustain animal progeny as well as provide food products for human consumption, and (3) the species-specific behavior of the animals, which places certain limitations on herd-composition and management as well as on productive capacity.

Reproductive and Productive Limitations

The greater the number of stock species raised by a population, the greater the capacity to exploit a particular habitat through selective grazing. However, different animals require different grazing strategies and different human-animal ratios for their care. Generally, the more types of animals raised, the larger the working force necessary to care for them, and we would expect to find more elaborate mechanisms of management cooperation in societies approaching a full-stock complex. The reproductive capacities of sheep, goats, and other members of the *Bovidae* are governed by the number of oestrus periods per year, the number of young per birth, and the knowledge of herding-management related to mating practices. In the case of sheep, the yearly increase potential has been reported in one setting as 40 percent.[9] Survival rates depend on nutrient and disease factors, as well as skilled management which incorporates the behavioral needs of the animals.

Productive capacity depends on factors such as seasonal variation in availability of pastures and water, as well as management techniques. Selective breeding results from an emphasis on one product or ability over others, such as milk over meat, or riding camels over transport, etc.; in many cases such selective breeding is responsive to the market demands of the larger economic system. In the ethnographic literature, there is very little statistical material on the relative use of animals for subsistence, for market, and as a medium of exchange, and much more needs to be known about the ways in which pastoral nomads use their animals. We would expect that one of the common features of all nomadic systems is the balance that must be maintained between the use of animals for subsistence and their use as capital.

Optimization of Productive Efficiency

Various practices serve to optimize the productive efficiency of herd animals. Though herding techniques are myriad, a number of conditions must be met in order to use animals for subsistence. One of these is the proper care of animal progeny, and it is evident from our material from Baluchistan that management techniques geared to increase the herd and to protect progeny are varied and complex. For example, it is a general practice to separate lambs and kids from their mothers after a short suckling period (so that the ewes will not reject their young).

They are not reintroduced into the main herd until the end of the fourth month, when the majority of males have been castrated. This procedure seems to result not so much from the fact that the young would directly exhaust the milk supply intended for human consumption (as the Brahui believe), but from the fact that lactating ewes tend to separate themselves off with their young from the main flock when the young are present, making the herd more difficult to control and thus limiting grazing activity. This would result in a decrease in milk yield.

Another technique, seen specifically among the Brahui, is an attempt to maintain an "optimal" herd size--a range within which the herd may vary without decreasing its grazing efficiency.[10] Some of the factors setting both upper and lower limits to herd size should be considered at this juncture since they have a direct bearing on forms of social organization.

The most obvious limitation on flock size is the availability of personnel to care for the animals. In most nomadic societies, the nuclear or elementary family (in its various phases of stem extension) is the unit of production and consumption, and the animals are owned by the component members, who make decisions about their deployment and general welfare. The family must allocate its working force (and sometimes hired help) to the various activities which it performs, and it maximizes its returns by joining with other families in various kinds of cooperative activities. Thus, flock size is a function of the relationship between numbers of animals, available working personnel (as determined by work roles), and the carrying capacity of local areas. In the Sarawan area of Baluchistan, the upper limit to flock size is 500 animals. Brahui households combine their animal holdings into joint flocks, often with hired herdsmen, for it is believed that 500 is the maximum number which can be efficiently grazed by one shepherd with the aid of a dog. Since the number of sheep/goats varies greatly from household to household, families combine their holdings into large flocks and form camps on a contractual basis for a period of a year. So strong is the obligation to remain in a flock/camp complex (khalk) once an agreement is made, and so rational are the choices made in the formation of flocks, that I have argued elsewhere that camps take shape around the formation of flocks.[11] While the structural principles of camp formation are the familiar agnation and affinality, the shifts which take place in camp membership from year to year represent adjustments in the formation of the most expedient sheep/goat flocks as grazing units.

In addition to an upper limit to flock size, the Brahui also recognize a minimum flock size of approximately 250 animals, and recruitment to camps is geared to keep the flock above this number. One informant recounted his experience in this way:

> Last year I was in Haji M. Karim's camp. The year before that I was in Khoda Ram's camp. We change a lot depending on whether we have few or many sheep. Last spring (hatām) I had only thirty-five sheep, and I asked EK if I could join his camp (khalk). Large flocks are no good, and M. Karim has a large one now. It is also not good when a man has a small number [of animals]. EK's flock is smaller [than Haji M. Karim's].

Barth describes a similar concern of the Basseri of south Persia in keeping flock size above a minimum number, but he does not consider any of the factors involved in setting a lower limit. He reports: "A shepherd is readily able to control a herd of up to four hundred head and there is some feeling that very small herds are relatively more troublesome."[12]

For the Brahui, one apparent reason for keeping flocks as close to 500 animals as possible is the competition for herdsmen. The use of a professional herdsman allows the men of the camp to engage in the labor market of the surrounding towns and villages--an important source of cash and wheat (especially for those with few animals). In contrast to the Basseri, where the animal holdings per tent-household are reported to be much larger than among the Brahui, and the herdsmen are often adolescent boys of the household rather than skilled tent-heads, the Brahui herdsman is often an adult male who is responsible for the animals of many tents. Each camp, then, competes to attract herdsmen with reputations for reliability and knowledge about grazing. A herdsman will naturally choose the camp with the largest flock up to 500, for his remuneration is based on the number of animals he herds. Camps whose herds fall substantially below 500 animals cannot attract herdsmen with proven skill.[13]

An additional factor in setting a lower limit to flock size is the relationship between flock size and grazing efficiency. Brahui informants report that when a sheep flock falls below 250 animals, it becomes more difficult to herd and the animals fare less well than they do in larger flocks.[14] They "waste away," as the Brahui express it. There are at present no data on flock size and grazing efficiency in free-ranging conditions, but the fact that the Brahui, as well as other groups, are uneasy with small flocks leads us to suspect that a lower limit may be a critical variable in nomad economy for reasons other than a minimum number being needed to support a family.

Dispersal and Conversion

The two main mechanisms for maintaining animal/pasture/personnel balances are dispersal and conversion. Disperal involves temporary movement of animal stock to other flocks and villages in return for their care, and also the purchase of animals in partnership. In the first instance, the borrower is entitled to both the produce and the progeny of his borrowed animals, while the owner profits from reduced numbers and the chance to disperse his holdings against severe losses from drought or disease. The purchase of animals in partnership is a mechanism for putting cash to work for investors who have been successful in building large herds, while at the same time providing subsistence stock for herdsmen with few animals. The investor realizes a profit when the animals are sold in market, while the small herdsman (who originally provided no cash for the purchase) cares for the animals and gains a chance to build up his herd. This kind of investment gives the investor access to many animals without his having to care for them or worry about their effect on the composition of the camp; they are truly "cash on the hoof."

One of the most common patterns of dispersal among the Brahui, and of particular interest when considering interaction between nomads and villagers, is the practice of placing animals with trusted friends (anāmat) in villages and transhumant hamlets. By this practice, the nomad quickly and temporarily reduces his stock, while at the same time strengthening trade relations with particular villagers. The villager enjoys the use of the animals for the tenure of the agreement and shares no responsibility for loss or injury. There are, of course, important implications in this practice for the development of shared cultural expectations, for it is one of the key points at which the nomad and sedentary systems articulate.

Conversions are transfers of stock wealth into other forms of wealth, such as partnerships in irrigation complexes, jewelry, and (recently) land. Stock are also converted into bride-wealth (lab), to make obligatory payments on occasions of sorrow (pūrs), as well as payments at times of joy (bijjār), to show hospitality, as in the slaughter of animals in honor of guests, to religious sacrifices (khairāt), and to other forms of prestige. In the Middle East, there is considerable variation in cultural practices relating to conversions, both in the relative liquidity of stock wealth and in market practices involving animal products. Barth reports concerning south Persia:

> The only other imperishable form of wealth into which wealth in flocks can be converted in the traditional South Persian economy is land. . . . There is an active market in landed property in the area. . . . [S]uch property can be freely subdivided and transferred to any buyer. . . . The typical pattern for wealthy nomads is therefore to convert a fraction of their wealth in flocks into landed property.[15]

In Baluchistan, especially in Kalat, land became available for purchase only quite recently. Both nomads and villagers are tribally organized, and there is not the traditional association of nomads with tribalism and landed peasants with cultivation that we find in Iran and elsewhere. Cultivable land is held by tribal sections as jagīr--land and/or water that was assigned to tribal sections (and sometimes individuals) by the Khan of Kalat and is not subject to revenue. Alienation of jagīr land is strictly defined by tribal norms, among which is a clear proscription against sale. At the present time, however, jagīr holdings are being sold, but on a limited scale and not without the scorn of agnates.

The variability in the sale of stock by-products is clearly a determinative aspect of pastoral economy. Among the Marri Baluch there is a strict cultural prohibition against the sale of milk, lest an animal in the herd die.[16] While the Brahui consume their own milk and generally do not sell milk in market, there is no proscription against its sale. (Much data remain to be collected regarding the type and quantity and seasonal variability in sale of stock products in market.)

There are also cultural limitations on consumption. Those who have worked among nomadic people know that animals are not slaughtered indiscriminately for the dinner table. In fact, meat is never a staple in the nomad's diet. Naturally, where animals are capital as well as repositories of wealth, their conversions are handled with great care lest the stock become depleted. All nomads are faced with the possibility of severe losses due to desiccation and disease. The occasions on which animals are slaughtered are prescribed by Islam and accord with sacrifices and norms of hospitality.

Various institutions and group types facilitate processes of conversion and dispersal. We have already cited the confederacy as a type of organization serving to stabilize territory, especially in environments of great ethnic diversity and/or nomadic competition. We also noted that the family was an important unit of social structure, an autonomous unit of production and consumption. However, because the adaptive processes involved in animal husbandry require balances between stock, personnel to manage them, other forms of assets, and deployment to pastures or stubble fields, families cannot maximize the required balances without cooperation. The internal structure of the tribe--both in terms of residential groups, such as families, herding units, camps, and camp groups, and the principles of social organization which define membership in lineages, "clans," and sections--is an accommodation to the exigencies of nomadism.

I have argued elsewhere[17] that the camp, as a group type, is an adaptive response to pastoral technology, mediating balances between pasture availability, the animal population, and the human population throughout the year. In pastoral life, the number of personnel necessary for the care of animals varies with the animals' productive cycle. When herds are in milk, they are usually in close association with camps, and there is a high demand for cooperative labor. However, when herds are dry (and for many nomads this may be for many months at a time), camps and herds are often separated by many miles, and the demands for working personnel and for cooperative structures are at a minimum. Thus the yearly cycle of production becomes an important variable in considering the functions of groups, as well as the potential for nomads to engage in the labor market.

The principle of agnation, which is expressed in the formation of groups between the level of the family and the tribe--i.e., sections and sub-sections, "clans," "co-liable" groups (as Emanuel Marx calls them)[18]--may also be seen as providing a framework for the maintenance of requisite balances. The mutual obligations between agnates concerning animal and cash contributions (known among the Brahui as bijjār, or obligatory contributions), as well as other institutions within which animal wealth is dispersed and converted, such as zaka', anticipatory inheritance, bride-wealth, and those dictated by the norms of hospitality, can all be considered in terms of their adaptive functions. Through anticipatory inheritance, a man can siphon off his stock over a period of time by allocating them to sons of marriageable age. Indeed, whether or not the sons remove their animals from the flock at marriage often depends on the flock's size. The time between betrothal and marriage is often many years, during which time bride-wealth is transmitted and other kinds of gifts are exchanged between the two families who will be joined in marriage. It is thus fruitful to consider some of the latent functions of nomad institutions as an integral part of nomad technology and economy.

We have attempted in this discussion to elaborate the traditional model of pastoral nomadic adaptation which deals with balances between pastures, animals, and humans. We see the animal population being determined by biological constraints in the form of reproductive capacity and species-specific flock behavior which sets upper and lower optima regarding flock size. We have found it necessary to deal in terms of a larger ecosystem than is ordinarily treated, since economic practices such as hired herdsmen, marketing of animals and/or their products, day labor at agricultural settlements, etc., affect the allocation of labor within the domestic unit and its particular constellation of resources and conversion alternatives. The facilitation of these economic behaviors involving synchronic contact between nomadic and settled populations, and the ease with which a nomadic group can move along the nomadic-sedentary continuum, are functions of more inclusive forms of sociopolitical integration.

We now consider the diachronic process and the constraints introduced when nomads begin to cultivate. We address ourselves to two main questions: (1) What happens when nomads begin to cultivate, combining dry-crop cereal production with stock raising in free-ranging conditions? (2) What are the consequences of incorporating a double-cropping cycle into cultivation when irrigation is introduced?[19] Here, I will rely heavily on our data concerning the Kalat district of Baluchistan.

The transhumant population of the Kalat Plateau are engaged in both herding and farming. Their yearly migration, not unlike that of the nomads, is the alternate use of highlands which lie at elevations between 5,000 and 7,000 feet, and the Kachhi plain, which is at sea level and nowhere rises above 500 feet. In the highlands of Sarawan and Jhalawan, the transhumants live in permanent hamlets and practice cultivation and herding, while in the plains they are indistinguishable from the nomads--living in tents, grazing their animals, and working as day laborers harvesting sorghum in the surrounding fields. By their simultaneous maintenance of flocks composed of sheep and goats, and their use of camels for transport and draught purposes (plowing, turning water wheels, threshing, etc.), they have developed an alternating system of yearly production which we call the transhumant niche.

The Kahnak valley of Kalat (including Dulai) first came under the control of the Brahui when the Khan of Kalat was granted the area by Ahmad Shah Abdalli, the Durrani king of Kabul (c. 1747), in return for military services rendered in his conquest of Delhi. The Khan of Kalat assigned the territory to the Raisani tribe as jagīr, or revenue-free grant, and the Raisanis then offered tenancy contracts (latbundi) to sections of tribes who were allied with them in battle. Thus, Kahnak (and Dulai) is held as jagīr by various agnatic lineages of the Raisani tribe, who hold proprietary rights, while other tribes and sections (such as the Summalari, Sumalzai, Sheikh Husseini, Mohamed Shahi, *et al.*) hold tenancy contracts with the Raisanis and pay one fourth of the crop from dry fields and one sixth of the irrigated crop from Persian-wheel wells. These tenant hamlets are composed of patrilineal local descent groups, who hold their contracts by virtue of agnatic descent down to the component households. Under the tenancy contract, the cultivator has complete freedom in the choice and amount of crops planted, and in the organization of production. He supplies seed, draught animals, agricultural implements, and labor. He may, if he wishes, sell his right, lease it (hijara), or engage a subtenant (buzghar) without permission from the Raisani proprietary group. In the case of sale, members of the same local descent group have the first right of purchase, while the second right is held by cultivators of bordering fields, reflecting the lien on cultivation rights held by closely related agnatic lineages.

ADAPTIVE PROCESSES REGULATING NOMAD-SEDENTARY INTERACTION

On the following pages I have presented the transhumant subsistence cycle in table form to show the alternation of resources and the resulting constraints. "One-crop" refers to a single cropping during the year in which no well irrigation is used, thus producing only one cereal crop (mainly wheat and some barley) along with a subsidiary dry-tract melon harvest in the fall. There are many small hamlets in the hills with anywhere between five and 25 families who single-crop on dry tracts. The double-cropping cycle ("two-crop") requires irrigation, and depends on the use of either Persian-wheel wells, diesel-machine wells, or *qanats* (called locally by the Persian word *karez*). Because karez-irrigated villages are inhabited by high ranking tribal sections, such as the Raisanis, holding proprietary rights to large tracts of land with few animal holdings, they are not considered transhumant as defined here.

As can be seen from the table, early spring (*hatām*) marks the return of the transhumants to their highland hamlets from their winter encampments in the plains. The return migration is scheduled to coincide with the availability of green pasturage in the hills. Scouts are often sent on ahead to determine if the growth of grasses is adequate for movement. The transition from plains to hills is precarious, for the flock has recently dropped its young and is now in milk and must have access to green pastures to sustain the flow. As soon as they reach their hamlets, those families who practice double-cropping can fodder-feed their animals on stalks cut from *walaiti* wheat which was planted the previous November, as well as on alfalfa, the only crop grown specifically for fodder.[20] All transhumants, however, carry with them sacks of sorghum grain from their harvest work in the plains, for the wheat from the previous June harvest has long since been depleted, and they must rely on sorghum *chapattis* (*dodi*) and milk products until the June harvest. In March, *shorawaki* wheat fields are prepared and planted, and by April, families who double-crop sow spices and plant small subsistence gardens of vegetables and tobacco. In late April and May, autumn crops such as watermelons and musk melons are sown on irrigated tracts, followed by potatoes and onions. All during this time, the herds are grazed in pastures surrounding the hamlets and are prohibited from entering only newly planted wheat fields. Milk and milk products now form the subsistence base, since the sorghum grain brought up from the plains is now depleted. Families might purchase flour in local towns using cash derived from the sale of animals in market, but they are reluctant to buy in large quantities because June wheat will soon be available.

By early June, both varieties of wheat are ready for harvest. The valley floor begins to lose its green hue, and the drying vegetation begins to have its effect on the quantity of milk produced by the flocks. From mid-July until lambing time in December and January, no milk is available, and although

TRANSHUMANT

Month	Season	Location	Natural Vegetation
March	hatām (karrai)	HIGHLANDS	Valley in bloom; rain expected
April			Valley green
May			
June	bashām		Grasses drying
July	tirma		Grasses dry
August			
September	sohēl		
October			
November	selh	Migration PLAINS 500 ft.	
December			
January			Fresh vegetation
February		Return migration	

SUBSISTENCE CYCLE

Cultivation Activity		Animals
One-Crop	Two-Crop	
Wheat sowing (*shorawaki*)	Wheat sowing (*shorawaki*) Alfalfa watering Spice sowing (coriander and cumin) Small subsistence gardens of vegetables and tobacco planted	Heavy grazing Milk available Young kept in separate flock Animals (castrated sheep and goats) sold in market
Watermelons planted (*kutikh*)	Watermelons and musk melons (*galau*) Plant potatoes, onions	
Wheat harvest (*shorawaki*)	Wheat harvest (*shorawaki*) (*walaiti*) Pruning and watering autumn crops	Lambs and he-goats castrated Young introduced into main flock Little milk Supplementary fodder (*pug*) Shearing Browsing on wheat stubble No milk
Melon harvest		Browsing on melon stubble
	Plowing and irrigating for winter wheat (*walaiti*) Wheat (*walaiti*) planting Onion harvest Potato harvest	
		No milk
Reaping in Kachhi villages		Grazing on Kachhi vegetation Stubble grazing (*nar*)
Sorghum harvest ends		Supplementary fodder (sorghum and pulses) Lambing Grazing over short distances Milk available Shearing Separate flock for young

certain kinds of stored cheeses are eaten, the bulk of the diet consists of wheat, lentils purchased in stores, and collected wild grasses and mushrooms.

In October, households that single-crop prepare to take their flocks to the plains which, by now, are grazing at ever greater distances from hamlets in search of pasturage. Where irrigation and double-cropping have been introduced, however, the autumn harvest has provided stubble fields which allow adequate grazing until departure for the plains, and there have been increasing delays in departure over the years. Families who double-crop and still maintain large flocks can migrate to the plains only after the potato harvest in November and after the merchants on consignment have taken the autumn crop to market.

It is apparent from this short descriptive account of the transhumant cycle that the process of sedentarization has significant economic consequences. The new constraints are manifest in new patterns of social organization. First, and most apparent, is stabilized access to cultivable tracts through tenancy contracts, mentioned earlier. In contrast to nomad camps, which are not homologous with lineages, the transhumant hamlet gives rise to the localized descent group, since the tenant contracts are held by virtue of membership in agnatic lineages. The hamlet places a community boundary around agnatic lineages that never comes into being in nomad camp structure. The face-to-face community is now fixed with permanent members and no longer has, or needs, the structural capacity to expand and contract in response to nomadic requirements.

In terms of traditional nomadic economics, the ready access to wheat and other grain staples, which no longer have to be purchased throughout the year, has important implications for stock holdings. The number of animals that have to be sold in market to raise cash for various purchases is now reduced. At the same time, the number of animals per flock is reduced because of the diminished carrying capacity of hill areas when the flocks are in milk and cannot be grazed more than half a day's walk from their home hamlet if they are to return each night for milking.[21] Transhumant flocks, in contrast to nomad flocks, have many more goats than sheep, which might be explained by the fact that the food requirements of goats can, under transhumant conditions, be met more readily than those of sheep. Although sheep's milk is richer in fat content than goat's milk, and is therefore capable of yielding more clarified butter per unit, goats give more milk than sheep. As a result, the transhumant flock can be kept smaller than nomad flocks without decreasing the daily supply of milk.

Probably the most important difference between transhumant and nomadic economies is the ready access of transhumants to money derived from cash crops. With the introduction of irrigation technology, the double-cropping niche came into being, with its capacity for intensive cultivation, but at the same time it brought greater demands for investments in equipment and seed, and in labor demands. (I have argued elsewhere that one of the ways of balancing labor demands [working personnel] with capital assets [animals, rights to cultivation, etc.] is to stabilize extended family households.)[22]

Our records clearly indicate a high correlation between extended families and well-irrigation which contrasts sharply with the predominance of elementary family structure among the nomads. We also found evidence that there is a higher incidence of actual FBD (father's brother's daughter) marriage in extended family households with double-cropping estates than in elementary families within the same hamlet which have no access to irrigation. While endogamy is high in elementary families, we found that the spouses are more distant agnates than patrilateral parallel cousins. When we compared this data to nomadic sections, we also found a high incidence of endogamy, but a lower incidence of actual FBD marriage when compared to more distant agnates. Thus, in terms of increasing labor demands with the development of irrigation technology, transhumant endogamy--specifically, the high incidence of actual FBD marriage--appears to be a structural attempt to keep members of a family tied to a specific household estate at critical phases in its developmental cycle.[23] The pooling of resources and cooperation among families with access to well-irrigation selects for the extended family household within this natural and social environment.

In the northern valleys of eastern Baluchistan, the process of sedentarization and the incorporation of a transhumant pattern was, it appears from census records, a stable niche. Populations plied between the nomadic and transhumant ways of life in response to variability in rainfall and water from wells. However, the introduction of diesel machines in the early 1960's and the growing capacity to tap sub-surface water has now begun a process of capitalization that is leading to complete settlement, and we are beginning to see concomitant structural changes in social organization.

Machine complexes are organized on the basis of contiguous fields and have the capacity to irrigate many more acres than Persian-wheels can (six acres, on the average). As a result, lineages are combining their constituent household holdings into single corporate complexes. The capital outlay for the installation of a 20 h.p. machine with a four-inch pipe diameter along with other equipment is sometimes made by investors from neighboring towns and villages in return for shares of produce and cash earned from their sale. The tremendous increase in productive capacity along with redeployment of working personnel has resulted in a system (as observed in 1968) which is clearly incompatible with the transhumant pattern. Families are no longer migrating to the plains, having sold most of their animal stock, and now remain in hamlets the year round. The increase in total crops and their subsidiary use as fodder has led to the replacement of camels by bullocks as draught animals. For the first time, these valleys can support a population the year round along with the draught animals necessary for labor-intensive cultivation. In 1968 the government was extending loans for the purchase and installation of electrical pumps at the same time that power lines were being run through the valleys. The commitment to sedentarization through land capitalization will ultimately link the hamlets to the larger market economy, as long as the water holds out. Unlike the transhumant pattern, which incorporated small-scale well-irrigation and allowed migration to the plains every year to protect the animal stock, the new pattern will not tolerate large animal holdings--indeed they are no longer viewed as a valuable source of capital investment. And unlike the transhumants, who could shift between nomadic movement and cultivation in response to seasonal and yearly variations in precipitation, the new villager, as an incipient peasant, is caught in his hill village and in the larger economic community.

Footnotes

[1] While adaptation to arid conditions by living organisms takes many forms, the striking fact in the study of desert life is the degree of convergent evolution that has taken place, producing common characteristics in many unrelated groups. (See J.L. Cloudsley-Thompson and M.J. Chadwick, Life in Deserts [Philadelphia: Dufour Publishing Co., 1964]).

[2] Fredrik Barth, Nomads of South Persia (Boston: Little, Brown and Co., 1961); Robert Pehrson, The Social Organization of the Marri Baluch (Chicago: Aldine Publishing Co., 1966); Robert Paine, "Herd Management in Northern Lapp Society" (paper prepared for Symposium 24 on Pastoral Nomadism, July 1964).

[3] Barth, Nomads of South Persia, p. 113.

[4] "Pasture" refers to natural vegetation grazed by herds under free-ranging conditions. "Pasturage" is used here to refer to prepared fodder, stubble grazing, and any other means of feeding herd animals involving human intervention in the preparation of food.

[5] Daniel Bates reports that for the Sacikara Yoruk "all their available pasture falls within village borders" and "rights to grazing are largely conditioned by contractual relations arrived

at with sedentary land-owners" ("Differential Access to Pasture in an Egalitarian Nomadic Society: The Sacikara Yoruk of Southeastern Turkey," paper read at meeting of American Anthropological Association, New Orleans, November 1969).

[6]Fredrik Barth, "The Land Use Pattern of Migratory Tribes of South Persia," Norsk Geografisk Tidsskdift, Bind XVII (1959-60), p. 5.

[7]Talal Asad, The Kababish Arabs (New York: Frederick Praeger, 1970), p. 21. There seems to be some confusion in Asad's account of pastures and water. On p. 13 he reports that named clans do not possess any rights to pastures and water: "Legally every Kababish has right of access to any pasture and water-point within the District so long as no damage is done by his animals to existing cultivations." On p. 21, he reports: "Neither watering points nor grazing grounds are individually or sectionally owned. Even prior occupation gives no exclusive rights of usufruct." On p. 27, however, we find that "rights to use of water is by traditional access and . . . these rights are held by individuals." I assume he means this to apply to damars ("restricted summer grazing grounds") only, although nowhere is this made clear.

[8]We might look for correlations in the nomadic literature between types of land tenure and the number and density of competing populations. In many animal species, we often find strong defense of territory where there is intense competition for resources within the same area.

[9]Barth, "The Land Use Pattern . . .," p. 71.

[10]Data on the behavior of sheep provide some suggestive leads, such as experimental work demonstrating the effect of allelomimetic behavior (the mutual imitative behavior of sheep which allows man to herd them) on grazing behavior. In one experiment, two groups of grazing sheep were used, one of which had its diet supplemented with food concentrates. It was observed that when the two groups grazed separately, the supplemented group spent less time in grazing than did the unsupplemented one, but when the two groups grazed together, the grazing and resting times for both groups were similar--demonstrating an increase in ingestive behavior for the supplemented animals when placed in a group of unsupplemented free-rangers. (See W.W. Swidler and N.B. Swidler, "Changes in the Relationship Between Men and Herd Animals with Increasing Sedentarization in Baluchistan," paper delivered at the American Association for the Advancement of Science meeting, Washington, D.C., December 1966).

[11]See W.W. Swidler, "Some Demographic Factors Regulating the Formation of Flocks and Camps Among the Brahui of Baluchistan,"

International Studies in Sociology and Social Anthropology, Journal of Asian and African Studies, Vol. VII, Nos. 1-2, January and April 1972.

[12] Barth, Nomads of South Persia, p. 22.

[13] The variability in minimum sheep/goat stock per family as reported by various authors (60 adult sheep for the Basseri, 40-50 for the Kababish, 30 or less for the Brahui) can best be explained by their respective roles in the nomadic economy. Among the Basseri, cash income is mainly derived from the sale of wool, butter, and hides, and not the animals themselves. Barth reports: "Animals may be freely sold, but the market for livestock is severely restricted" ("Capital, Investment and the Social Structure of a Pastoral Nomad Group in South Persia" in Raymond Firth and B.S. Yamey, eds., Capital, Savings and Credit in Peasant Societies [Chicago: Aldine Publishing Co., 1964], p. 73). In contrast, the Brahui derive much of their cash income from the sale of livestock, and it is therefore not uncommon to see elementary families with less than 30 adult sheep/goats. With the Kababish, who also derive their main cash income from the sale of livestock, larger sheep holdings per family than the Brahui may result from the fact that they participate less in the labor market and do not readily invest cash in assets other than animals (Asad, p. 30).

[14] Barth reports: "The Basseri say that sheep are not happy in too small groups; they spread and wander, and join larger herds; they will not move predictably, in a body." (Personal communication, August 1967).

[15] Barth, Nomads of South Persia, p. 104.

[16] Pehrson, p. 5.

[17] Swidler, "Some Demographic Factors . . . ."

[18] Emanuel Marx, Bedouin of the Negev (New York: Frederick Praeger, 1967), p. 63.

[19] The so-called double-cropping cycle permits two harvests during the year, allowing one cereal cropping and one vegetable harvest.

[20] In most of the hill areas, wheat is planted in two varieties: shorawaki and walaiti. Shorawaki is a three-month variety planted in February/March and harvested in June; it is a red wheat, and grows with little moisture on dry tracts. Walaiti, or "winter wheat," is a white, beardless variety planted on irrigated tracts and capable of greater per acre yields.

[21]An important variable in considering carrying capacities is the seasonal restraints on deployment of herds relative to their productivity. When dry, herds can be grazed at great distances from hamlets; when in milk, the distance is set by the need to return to home hamlets every night for milking.

[22]W.W. Swidler, "Technology and Social Structure in Baluchistan, West Pakistan" (Ph.D. dissertation, Columbia University, 1968), pp. 159-208.

[23]Among the Brahui, FBD marriage does not keep property within the family, as many believe is the case in the Arab Middle East. Females do not normally inherit, despite _Sharia_ prescriptions relating to female inheritance. Rather, _it keeps the family within the property (estate)_, especially at "structurally weak" times, when divisive processes such as inheritance and transitions in the developmental cycle of the family occur. When "family" is seen in the context of the developmental cycle, marriage choices have more structural meaning.

WOMEN AND POWER IN NOMADIC SOCIETIES OF THE MIDDLE EAST

Cynthia Nelson

Certain issues seem to me to be sorely neglected or simply taken for granted in most of the anthropological studies of the desert and the sown in the Middle East. I shall discuss these issues by raising the following questions:

1. What are some of the assumptions underlying the descriptions of the political significance of women in traditional Middle Eastern nomadic societies as reflected in ethnographic literature?

2. Can some of the factors associated with the distribution and exercise of power in nomadic societies be related directly to male and female roles?

3. What happens to men's and women's roles and the exercise of power in situations of sedentarization?

I shall begin by examining some of the assumptions relating to the man's and woman's social worlds in nomadic societies as expressed in specific ethnographic studies. (Insofar as it was possible I have utilized the published materials of those participating in this symposium for the purposes of stimulating discussion and eliciting further data on these issues.) I shall concentrate on the male image of the social worlds for the obvious reason that the ethnographic material on nomadic societies has been written almost exclusively by male anthropologists. Of the few descriptive and analytic accounts written by women (which tend to describe the sedentary situation), there is a suggestion that a great deal of what has been taken for granted about power and authority in nomadic society has been largely a reflection of "patriarchal politics," to borrow Kate Millett's term.[1]

The Male Image of Nomadic Women

In the monographs I have culled for statements descriptive of the social worlds in nomadic societies, I have discovered an interesting pattern. There is almost universal agreement among ethnographers that the nomadic setting is divided into two social worlds--the tent and the camp--in which the former is the private domain of the woman, and the latter is the public domain of the man. However, there is considerable disagreement as to the political significance of this phenomenon. Specifically, do nomadic women perform a "political" role, and if so--what and how?

The basic dichotomy between the two social worlds is reflected in the activities associated with each sphere. The tent is the domestic household, where family matters are handled, and the camp is the political arena, where decisions affecting the entire group are made. Women perform such tasks as food preparation and serving and milking goats, while the men are responsible for the care and maintenance of the major sources of production. However, it seems that when conditions necessitate, women are called upon to do men's work, but rarely the other way around. As Asad has said of the Kababish: "Whenever labour requirement is heavy, such as the annual migration cycle, women do men's work. . . . There is no male task that a woman may not perform . . . but men almost never perform women's tasks."[2] He observes that women are more often overworked than men, and that perhaps this leads to a reluctance of many women to part with their daughters. The Kababish division of the social worlds is described by Asad as follows:

> Most of an adult woman's time is spent at or near her tent carrying out an unending series of domestic duties and catering to the never ceasing demands of the men of her household. . . . When she moves the tent must be moved with her--and indeed by her, for dismantling, transporting and erecting the tent are primarily the responsibility of the woman. . . . In the absence of women, when men are away with the main herds or on a journey, many of these tasks (but never the grinding of grain) may be performed by men. But in the dar it would be considered shameful for them to do so. I have often seen men--and even young boys--standing and sitting idly near the household water skin call upon some woman who is otherwise busy to give them water to drink. For women must serve men, say the Kababish--lazim al-mara takhdim a r-ragil--Indeed since women and children have no sense, it is the responsibility of men to see that they perform their tasks properly. Since most of the female tasks are relatively uncomplicated and (more important) require little adult supervision, it is possible to make little girls work hard from a fairly early age. Young boys can not work alone at serious herding, which demands a high degree of skill and responsibility; comparatively less demand is therefore made on them than on their little sisters.[3]

In his study of the Basseri tribe of South Persia, Barth makes the point that the household is the basic, viable unit of nomad social organization, and notes that the man is completely dependent on the wife's willing cooperation in the daily routine of pastoral nomadism. She exercises considerable authority and autonomy in matters within the domestic sphere and family economics:

> With respect to decisions in the domestic and familial domain, men and women are more nearly equal and the distribution of authority between spouses is a matter of individual adaptation. Thus decisions regarding the multitude of choices in the field of production and consumption (but not decisions regarding migration routes and camp sites) and all matters of kinship, marriage, training of children and decisions that will greatly affect the family, such as whether to change one's group membership, or become sedentary--these are all decisions shared by the spouses and where the wiser predominates regardless of sex. . . . Thus the internal authority pattern of Basseri is similar to the urban Western family.[4]
>
> The strongly bilateral authority distribution that characterizes the domain and relations between close relatives can be extended in the political sphere within the camp without coming into conflict with explicit patrilineal authority.[5]
>
> As within the tent, where husband and wife are nearly equal in the domestic sphere (though husband is absolute head of the household in all external relations), so also within the camp: a bilateral system of duties and relations is obvious within the camp; while its outer boundaries are conceived in patrilineal terms, affinal relations serve to establish political bonds between tents.[6]

On the other hand, Asad asserts:

> In all households the ultimate responsibility of providing for dependents and the prerogative of making the final decisions about the management of household resources rests with the male head.[7]
>
> The overall authority of the household head is based on the fact that he has greater power and greater moral responsibility than any other member of the household.[8]
>
> Consent involves the recognition on the part of the Kababish in general that on the whole the leaders know what is best.[9]
>
> Women and children do not need any money--and if they get hold of some they just waste it. A man is responsible for buying all the requirements of his household--grain, tea, sugar, clothing, shoes. Women are irresponsible with money; they are just like children.[10]

Asad speaks in the name of the Kababish generally, but I suspect this is the view of his male informants. Similarly, Emanuel Marx displays the same tendency in his work on the Bedouin of the Negev:

> While the rights of women are fully recognized in the domestic sphere, Bedouin men are quite explicit that only men take part in political action in any form, and that only men become members of sections in a political sense.[11]

Marx emphasizes the same point when he says:

> A marriage link acts as a very effective communicative device between groups because the woman who conveys the communications is so intimately bound up with both her husband and sons and with her father and brothers. She has the interest of both groups at heart and would suffer most from an estrangement between the two groups. At the same time she is on the inside of both groups and thus able to assert her influence over the sections through the men to whom she is closely connected, as well as through women.[12]

Peters summarizes his view of Cyrenaican society as follows:

> Among semi-desert Bedouin, women were excluded from inheritance, but the degree of separation was relatively little and the use of the veil was situational only; their domestic status was high although they were excluded from the company of men; politically, marriage alliances were critical although women had virtually no say in the choice of spouse. . . . Of all the behavioral patterns which distinguish the sexes, the meal is perhaps the clearest and most rigid. Men cannot cook and women cannot herd. Men are not allowed to collect firewood; women are not allowed to plough or ride horses.[13]

These ethnographers all agree in their conception of Middle Eastern nomadic society as being structured in terms of two dichotomous social worlds--the private sphere of the tent (the woman's world) and the public sphere of the camp (the man's world). The prevalent assumption underlying this view of nomadic society is that the tent is the sphere of domestic life only; the camp is where political activity takes place, and women play no formal role in this political activity. However, the ethnographers disagree on the basic character of power and authority, as the quotations from Barth and Asad demonstrate. On the question "Do women exercise political power?" there is considerable variance.

What does it mean to distinguish between two social worlds and then argue that the only political activity is in the public sphere of the men? What attention has been paid by the ethnographers to the ways in which women influence public policy? From the literature we can glean certain hints as to how women can and do exercise political influence in the man's world, and thus point to the way this influence relates to male and female roles.

Women and the Exercise of Political Power

Peters summarizes the situation succinctly when he observes:

> The pivotal points in any field of power in this, a superficially dominant patrilineal, patrilocal and patriarchal society where the male ethos is vulgar in its brash prominence, are the women. What holds men together, what knots the cords of alliances are not men themselves, but the women who depart from their natal household to take up residence elsewhere with a man, and who, in this critical position, communicate one group to another.[14]

Peters argues that the division of work between the sexes has the consequence of giving both sexes rights in definable domains of life, and through them authority over members of the opposite sex. Men may boast of their dominance over women, but they are constrained in their actions by the control women possess over the preparation of food and the comforts of the shelter. Through the division of labor, women acquire rights in men and are able to exercise control over men in a way men cannot control them.

Men control the resources--land, water, animals, the durable properties; women control the products. Utilization of the products and the dividends derived from their use are granted to women, and through them they acquire legal claims on men. Women can make demands on men as a right and be given public support.

The fixity of groups of men to defined territorial areas is characteristic of Cyrenaica. By comparison, women are much more mobile and marry outside natal groups. Though they have no controlling rights in property, women nevertheless are critical in its manipulation. Bridewealth is the legal right to protection and support against the husband as the daughter or sister of the man who holds the bridewealth. The woman mediates the relations between the two men. The greater the bridewealth, the greater the political significance.[15]

Similarly, Cunnison points out, to a degree not found in most ethnographic literature written by men, that women play a significant informal role in the power careers of men among the Baggara Arabs. While women occupy no formal positions, they have a profound influence on politics in two respects:

1. They act as arbiters of men's conduct, and they can make or break a man's political career--singing songs of praise or mockery. Reputations are made or broken by women.
2. A policy decision that the men of a camp make is influenced by the kind of reaction that the women of the group are likely to have toward it.

In these respects, at least for the Baggara, women play a significant role in the struggle for power. As Cunnison points out:

> Cattle attract women and allow a man to marry more than one wife. The possession of cattle plays an important part in the relations of men and women. It implies that a man is endowed with those qualities that Baggara men and women alike regard as most admirable. Herd building means easier access to women, who play an instrumental part in spreading a man's virtue or challenging a man's honour. . . . Although there is often argument about amount of bridewealth to be paid, debate is not between the two families; instead the men of both families agree and unite in argument to try to beat down the price the bride's mother backed by the women of the family is demanding. Final word is that of the bride's mother. She can try to stop a marriage that she or her daughter don't want by refusing to lower the price. "Let us chase him off with our demands."[16]

Cunnison argues that the Baggara ideas about the nature of power and authority involve the closely related aims of wealth, women, and power,[17] and that manliness is also related to women, wealth, and power.[18]

Robert and Jean Pehrson, in their study of the Marri Baluch, ask the question: How can a woman in the structural position of subordination and isolation hope to defend her interests (and exert power over men)? They describe the three main tactics a woman uses to defend her interests: "playing men off against each other, seeking alliance and support from other women, and minimizing contact with her husband."[19] A mature woman can achieve much covert influence by playing her husband and her adult son off against each other or, in the case of agnatic marriage, by playing her brother(s) off against her husband. An awareness of this power is implicit in the Pehrson's ethnographic description of the advantages of agnatic cousin marriage and the strategy of marriage. The tactic of alliance of women in support of each other combines readily with the tactic of minimizing contacts with the husband.

Marri men see themselves as opposed by women--as fighting a continuous battle against female recalcitrance and laziness. Women even more markedly see themselves in a conspiracy of opposition against men. With the minimization of contact between spouses and an accommodation based on lack of knowledge of the activities of spouses, distrust tends to widen the schism. The general cultural milieu is a further contributing factor. In their relations to superiors, to strangers--to almost anyone--Marris expect to be manipulated and cheated, and tend to protect themselves by having only opportunistic transactions.

The image of nomadic society and hence of nomadic women we have from the literature is largely an image created by men. As one Marri woman poignantly stated:

> You know, it's all women's business--the giving or the stinginess, the helpfulness or the lack of helpfulness. What do men know about the household affairs? They are away from home a lot, they sleep under a rock at noon, or under a tree, rarely in their tents. <u>What do they know about what their women do</u>?[20]

We know very little about the woman's world as experienced and expressed by women. Of the literature I have been able to read by women about women in nomadic societies in the Middle East, a significant quantity is by Western travelers like Gertrude Bell, Lady Anne Blunt, and C. Colliver Rice, who sojourned among nomadic societies around the turn of the century and published descriptive letters and memoirs. For the most part these accounts are more interesting for what they reveal of the European image of the Muslim Middle East than they are informative about the specific issues with which we are dealing. An exception is the detailed and scholarly work of Ilse Lichtenstädter--<u>Women in the Aiyam Al-'Arab</u>--which offers an interesting analysis of the role the Arab woman played in the warfare of her tribe, and thus presents a view of the life and position of women in pre-Islamic Arabia.[21] Although the work deals with nomadic society during the Jahiliya, it is still informative about the manner in which Arab women behave in everyday life and how they exercise political influence in the man's world.

According to the Aiyam narratives, woman's influence was felt beyond the tent. Through marriage she played an important role in Arab policy by being the link and mediator through which powerful alliances between tribes were made. She acted as counselor to her son, who very often took her advice, and whenever possible she tried to gain influence over her son in order to bring an enmity to an end. Lichtenstädter points out:

> That Fatima bint al-Khurshub tried, though unsuccessfully, to mediate between her son and Qais b. Zuhair shows that she

could be sure that her opinion would at least be heard. In this case, however, the son did not accept his mother's advice; the events proved that she was right.[22]

In warfare the woman very often was the cause of quarrels and great feuds. She was also employed as a spy and, if captured in war, the source of great ransoms. Since the women were not far from where the battles took place, they were able to watch the fighting and incite their men by acclamations. When in great distress and danger, the Arabs had recourse to a device meant to excite their courage and their desire to fight to the highest degree: they exposed their women, particularly noble women, to danger by forcing them to fall from their camels and litters in order to show the warriors that they must fight to the death.[23]

In summarizing her analysis, Lichtenstädter suggests that pre-Islamic nomadic society was a society that treated women with esteem and allowed them to take part in public life:

> From the Aiyam tales pre-Islamic Arab women played a part in the life of their tribe and exercised an influence which they lost only later in the development of Islamic society. . . . But as during the time of Jahiliya women were not separated from men but lived in close intercourse with them, they could readily get to know their plans and projects. . . . In addition the conditions of life were such that in times of distress clever advice was eagerly accepted and followed regardless whence it came, even if offered by a woman. In this sense we are justified in speaking of the "influence" of a woman without exaggerating her importance in the public life of an Arab tribe.[24]

From these remarks it appears that an important factor relating to the distribution and exercise of power among women in nomadic society is the degree of Islamization and the consequent separation of man's and woman's worlds, with the resultant assumption that the woman is inferior and participates only minimally in the political domain of decision-making in her society. In those nomadic societies in which there is a greater adherence to customary than to shari'a law, women enjoy a higher legal status and are in a better position to influence political decisions.

In her work on the Awlad 'Ali of the western desert of Egypt, Safia Mohsen begins by outlining the commonly held view among the Awlad 'Ali concerning the legal status of women--that women are mentally inferior to men and that God preferred men over women in matters of correct judgment and good counsel.[25] With the exception of a few holy women from the Murabiteen tribes, women are as a rule excluded from participation in public duties.

Leadership on all levels is confined to men, as is mediation in dispute settlements. But as Mohsen is quick to point out:

> Participation in the public affairs of the society is only one index of the political position of an individual or a group. An individual or a group may be related to politics in two different yet related ways. First, he may be related to politics as a policy maker. Here his position is determined by the amount of participation in determining and implementing public goals. Second, he may be related to politics as subject to political decisions and activities; that is the nature of his legal rights.[26]

Within the area of legal rights we find an image of nomadic women which is somewhat different from that described by male ethnographers. By giving us an analysis of some of the legal rights given to women by the customary law of Awlad 'Ali (some of which are not given to women by the modern legal system), especially in the area of marriage and the family, and of the guarantees they have for such rights, Mohsen gives us an insight into the position of women, not only in the legal system of Awlad 'Ali, but in nomadic society as a whole. "For customary law gives women in certain respects a position equal to that of men."[27]

What is perhaps most interesting in Mohsen's account is the manner in which woman's rights are enforced--that is, the woman's ability to dissolve a marriage through a customary procedure described as the right of woman to "throw herself." A woman who does not desire to continue living with her husband can go to a respectable man in the community and "throw herself" over to him. By her throwing herself, the man becomes obliged to give refuge to the woman and to start negotiating with her husband to divorce her. Owing to the prestige of the man usually selected (omda [village headman] or holy man), the husband cannot object to the divorce, although he may demand the mahr (bride-price) back. Success or failure of this divorce procedure depends on the careful selection of the man upon whom the woman "throws herself." The frequency of the practice and the lack of stigma attached to it give the woman a status almost equal to that of a man.

Another aspect of the relationship between women and the exercise of power in nomadic societies is the position of woman in the religious and supernatural world. Mathea Gaudry, in La Femme Chaouia de l'Aurès, draws attention to the power that women can exert over men in their capacities as saints, sorceresses, magicians, and healers--a theme rarely touched upon in the ethnographic literature on Middle Eastern nomadic societies written by men.[28] The Auresian woman has, like the man, the cult of mzara--places sanctified by the passage of a saint; and the women, like the men, affiliate themselves with religious organizations. There is the interesting example of a female Marabout, Turkeyya:

> There existed a Marabout of great virtue named Turkeyya who was most pious and exerted a great influence on her many clients and adepts. There was also a male Marabout, Sidi Moussa, seeing that his authority had diminished with a number of his followers, felt peeved. He decided to put an end to this competition with his dangerous rival and he devised a simple plan to get rid of her. He appealed to one of his devouts and entrusted him to kidnap Turkeyya and marry her. As a Marabout can only enter into a family of Marabout, she lost, from this mis-marriage, all the authority she had.[29]

Sorcery is another means by which women can exert their influence over men in Chaouia society, and as a sorceress a woman has more power over a man than as a saint because of her ability to divine the future, enhance love, ward off evil, and cure illness. According to Gaudry: "It can be said that the superstitious fear of the woman which filled the Berber mind allowed the women to impose an inferior religion of which they are the priestesses, which is a response to a collective need."[30] All old women are more or less sorceresses. They teach women to prepare lotions which can "tame any man." Men fear sorceresses, and some forbid their wives to receive them. A sorceress has power over the man through the woman. According to a male Chaouia proverb:

> The child of male sex comes to the world with 60 <u>jnoun</u> in his body; the child of the female sex is born pure; but every year, the boy gets purified of a jinn, whereas the girl acquires one; and this is the reason that old women, 60 years and with 60 jnoun are sorcerers more malignant than the devil himself. Blind she sews more material, lame she jumps over rocks, and deaf she knows all the news.[31]

The degree to which nomad women exercise power over men through the medium of the supernatural world has not been the focus of much anthropological field research among Middle Eastern nomadic societies. With the exception of studies carried out among the Berber Moslems in Morocco,[32] the Kabyles in Algeria,[33] and the Senusi in Cyrenaica,[34] very little attention has been focused on nomad religious life. In fact, many anthropologists assume that there is a lack of ritual among nomads.[35] However, it is not my purpose to discuss this hypothesis, but to inquire if the lack of material on the issue of woman and the supernatural is a reflection of lack of interest on the part of the nomads or the ethnographers. Dr. Hasan El Shamy, an Egyptian folklorist, has told me that in the nomadic societies of the eastern and western deserts of Egypt, concerning which he has collected material reflecting images of women, they have rarely produced their own saints, but have utilized saints from the sedentary societies. In addition, he has analyzed a collection of saints' manifestations by Al-Nahbani and found that all female saints have an urban or sedentary origin. However, of the 1400 cases described, only 26 related to female saints. One female acquired sainthood through her son's piety; the rest achieved it through their own merit--i.e., by kindness, piety, dedication, and closeness to God.

Women and Sedentarization

Up to this point I have been concentrating on the relationship of women to power in nomadic societies, and have attempted to demonstrate that women wield political influence in the sense that they have control over many of the basic goods or realms that men are interested in, such as sons, honor, food, sex, and the supernatural. By virtue of her mediating role between man and the larger world, woman has far more influence outside the domestic realm of the tent than male ethnographers have heretofore suggested.

A final question that I wish to raise concerns the transformation of social worlds under conditions of sedentarization. That is, in what ways does the sedentary situation offer women opportunities for the exercise of power that may not be present in the nomadic situation?

Abdulla Bujra, in his research among the Awlad 'Ali of Mersa Matrouh, has pointed out that nomads who fall below a certain subsistence level are drawn to the villages, where they become peasants, but we do not know what significance women have in this movement toward the sown. In an article entitled "Relationship between the Sexes amongst the Bedouin in a Town," Bujra states that the role of Bedouin women has not changed much in the town, but the women are using the new situation to remedy a structural weakness in the marriage relationship.[36] The bride now takes a dowry to her husband. This dowry gives the woman a material stake in the new household. A husband would lose it by divorcing her, and is therefore (they say) likely to think twice before doing so. Thus, the movement to town has made divorce less likely. According to Bujra, both the men and women are assimilating only those aspects of the sedentary value system which give them advantages in the restructuring of relationships between the sexes. This suggests that there are significant transformations of the man's and woman's worlds, and that there are advantages accruing to women as well as men in settling down that deserve more detailed ethnographic analysis by those concerned with issues of the linkage between the desert and the sown.

Barth suggests that decisions about whether to become sedentary are shared by both spouses. His study indicates that among the Basseri the flow is overwhelmingly in the direction of sedentarization. One of the factors emphasized in the recruitment of settlers is the absence of numerous siblings and children, which secure a person's position in nomad society.[37]

From my own field observations in the settled Bedouin community of King Mariut, 54 kilometers west of Alexandria, it is evident that the women perform many more of the economic and productive roles in the community than in a nomad situation. In addition to the usual domestic tasks of cooking, cleaning, and caring for children, the women participate in agriculture (planting and harvesting barley), tending the flocks, raising chickens and rabbits for market, and preparing the fibers from sheep's wool for weaving rugs, which are later sold in the local market. The men, on the other hand, work almost exclusively as ghaffirs (guardians) to property rented or owned by Nile Valley Egyptians who come to King Mariut on holidays. In certain instances men own fig orchards but employ others--usually Maraboutin--to cultivate and harvest, since Awlad 'Ali men disdain horticulture. For the most part, the young men of the village make periodic migrations to Libya where they work as laborers for large oil companies. Anwar Khayreya supports this view of the increased economic and productive value of women in the sedentary situation in her study "The Women of El Hamam in the Western Desert."[38] She observes that women control the family budgets and have opportunities to increase their wealth through the sale of rugs, blankets, and jewelry, as well as poultry and eggs.

Barbara Aswad describes the increased political significance of women as groups become sedentarized. In her study of a plains village along the Turkish-Syrian border, she shows how certain women, substituting for men, have exercised direct economic and political influence as groups have become sedentarized.[39] Role shift occurs when a man dies leaving plural wives and small children; the widow who makes the role shift never remarries. Her authority and responsibility operate in the public sphere as follows:

1. She maintains children and other wives;

2. She controls significant amounts of land;

3. She engages in the making of political alliances through the arrangement of children's marriages and bride prices;

4. She contracts with sharecroppers and other village males; and

5. She works within the framework of her husband's system of alliances.

She is fully respected in this role by society. "She becomes like a man," as the villagers say approvingly. According to Aswad, 19 of 68 men of the landowning patrilineage had property controlled and managed by women for a period of up to ten years.

These cases give us important evidence of the increased economic and political significance of women in some situations of sedentarization. No claim is made that this is the trend in all cases of transition from desert to sown life styles, but it suggests further questions for research.

For example, what is the significance of the distinct separation of social worlds in nomadic and sedentary situations?[40] Does the development of landownership on a more private basis and the search for wage labor outside the village create greater opoportunities for women to exercise control in sedentarization?[41] How important are sainthood, sorcery, and magic as media through which women in sedentary societies exercise control over men? An examination of the ethnographic literature indicates that these are questions that have not been of much significance to male anthropologists.

Conclusion

The purpose of this paper has been to look at the ideas held about women in nomadic societies and their position in an avowedly man-centered world--not in order to determine women's "proper place," but to explore the images of women in nomadic society, as well as the assumptions of its investigators. I have been hopelessly eclectic in choosing my examples to highlight issues or suggest lines of inquiry. The main issue with which this paper has been concerned is: What are the implications for the development of our anthropological understanding of nomadic society when the data express predominantly a male perspective? Stated in somewhat different terms, what are the implications of the fact that male ethnographers have overwhelmingly been the interpreters of the social worlds of nomadic societies in the Middle East and North Africa (and perhaps of pastoral societies in general) for the kinds of models that have been developed in anthropology to analyze and discuss the desert and the sown?

It seems apparent to me that a majority of ethnographers (including several of the participants of this symposium) tend to think about nomadic society and political authority in terms of a game of strategies of how people in groups make decisions. One anthropologist expresses this approach as follows:

> The main sources of power and authority available to persons are ownership of land, the provision of hospitality and a

> reputation for honor. Most statuses and rights are usually defined by contractual agreements between persons. In these circumstances each man's aim may be seen as the adoption of the strategy that will best serve his interest.[42]

Given this statement, and given the evidence I have tried to muster in this paper concerning the point of view of male ethnographers--i.e., that women exercise little or no political power in nomadic societies--then this model is a reflection of a game that only men can play, and hence is very androcentric. It is also a reflection of how anthropologists tend to conceptualize power--as necessitating a public arena in the Greek polis sense, which is a Western conceptualization. If we understand politics to refer to power-structured relationships or arrangements whereby one group of persons is controlled by another, then I think we must, as Kate Millett has suggested, see the relationship between the sexes in a political context, and examine in detail the manner in which women exert influence on (and hence control) men and therefore participate in the power structure of society. Millett has suggested that "patriarchal politics" obtains consent through the "socialization" of both sexes to the basic patriarchal bias with regard to temperament, role, and status. From the ethnographic literature on nomadic society there is ample evidence to support the idea that the woman defines herself and her position in terms of values centered about the man. She then uses the male-centered value system to attain her own ends by way of manipulative techniques that force man to recognize female power without losing his self-esteem. The situation of the woman in nomadic societies seems analogous to what Asad describes as the relation between the elite and the masses among the Kababish:

> The masses (i.e. the women) accept the exclusive right of their rulers (i.e. males) to dominate, but their conception of this legitimacy derives from an understanding of their political predicament and not from indoctrination and therefore is not congruent with the conception of legitimacy which the elite (i.e. males) entertain.[43]

I shall close by quoting two traditional Arab proverbs that perhaps more than anything else indicate that within the symbolic world of man, woman is a power to be reckoned with:

> If a man is a sea, a woman must be his dam.
>
> Women can be defeated only by death.

Footnotes

[1]Kate Millett, Sexual Politics (New York: Doubleday, 1970).

[2]Talal Asad, The Kababish Arabs: Power, Authority and Consent in a Nomadic Tribe (London: C. Hurst and Co., 1970).

[3]Ibid., pp. 44-45. [All emphases in this and other quotations in this article are mine--C.N.]

[4]Fredrik Barth, Nomads of South Persia: Basseri Tribe of the Khameseh Confederacy (Boston: Little Brown and Co., 1961), pp. 15-16.

[5]Ibid., p. 41.

[6]Ibid., pp. 38-39.

[7]Asad, p. 37.

[8]Ibid., pp. 100-101.

[9]Ibid., p. 237.

[10]Ibid., p. 93.

[11]Emanuel Marx, Bedouin of the Negev (New York: Praeger, 1967), p. 186.

[12]Ibid., p. 157.

[13]Emrys Peters, "Consequences of the Segregation of the Sexes Among the Arabs" (paper delivered at the Mediterranean Social Science Council Conference, Athens, 1966), p. 1.

[14]Ibid., p. 15.

[15]Ibid., p. 18.

[16]Ian Cunnison, The Baggara Arabs: Power and Lineage in a Sudanese Nomad Tribe (Oxford: Clarendon Press, 1966), pp. 116-117.

[17]Ibid., pp. 115ff.

[18]Ibid., p. 176.

[19]Robert and Jean Pehrson, The Social Organization of the Marri Baluch (Viking Fund Publication in Anthropology, No. 43, 1966), p. 59.

[20]Ibid., p. 75.

[21]Ilse Lichtenstädter, Women in the Aiyam Al-'Arab (London: The Royal Asiatic Society, 1935).

[22] *Ibid.*, p. 65.

[23] *Ibid.*, p. 43.

[24] *Ibid.*, pp. 81, 83, and 85.

[25] Safia Mohsen, "Legal Status of Women Among the Awlad 'Ali," *Anthropological Quarterly*, Vol. 40, No. 3 (1967), pp. 153-166. Reprinted in Louise Sweet, ed., *Peoples and Cultures of the Middle East*, Vol. I (New York: Natural History Press, 1970).

[26] *Ibid.*, p. 153.

[27] *Ibid.*, p. 155.

[28] Mathea Gaudry, *La Femme Chaouia de l'Aurès* (Paris: Geuthner, 1929).

[29] *Ibid.*, p. 235.

[30] *Ibid.*, p. 246.

[31] *Ibid.*, p. 267.

[32] Vincent Crapanzano, "The Hamadsha" in Nikki R. Keddie, ed., *Scholars, Saints and Sufis: Muslim Religious Institutions since 1500* (Berkeley: University of California Press, 1970).

[33] Robert Montagne, *La Vie sociale et la vie politique des Berbères* (Paris, 1931).

[34] E. Evans-Pritchard, *The Sanusi of Cyrenaica* (Oxford: Clarendon Press, 1949).

[35] Barth, *Nomads of South Persia*, Appendix, 135.

[36] Abdullah Bujra, "The Relationship between the Sexes amongst the Bedouin in a Town" (paper delivered at the Mediterranean Social Science Council Conference, Athens, 1966).

[37] Barth, *Nomads of South Persia*, pp. 113-121.

[38] Anwar Khayreya, "The Women in El Hamam in the Western Desert" (thesis for diploma of the Institute of Social Sciences, University of Alexandria, Egypt, 1969).

[39] Barbara Aswad, "Key and Peripheral Roles of Noble Women in a Middle East Plains Village," *Anthropological Quarterly*, Vol. 40, No. 3 (1969), pp. 139-152.

[40] See Peters.

[41]Henry Rosenfeld, "The Contradictions Between Property, Kinship and Power as Reflected in the Marriage System of an Arab Village" in J. Peristiany, ed., Contributing to Mediterranean Sociology (The Hague: Mouton, 1968), pp. 247-260.

[42]Fredrik Barth, Political Leadership among the Swat Pathans (London School of Economics Monographs on Social Anthropology, No. 19, 1959).

[43]Asad, p. xvi.

THE BEDUIN AS A MILITARY FORCE: NOTES ON SOME ASPECTS OF POWER RELATIONS BETWEEN NOMADS AND SEDENTARIES IN HISTORICAL PERSPECTIVE

Talal Asad

This essay consists of notes on the socioeconomic conditions which define the military significance of nomads in relation to sedentary populations within the Arab Middle East. An attempt will be made to explore some fundamental dimensions of the problem by using historical material.

The vast historical literature on Arab nomads is filled with references, both general and specific, to the warlike propensities of beduins. Classical Arabic literature on pre-Islamic society--the Jahiliyya--is largely an account of intertribal battles and military exploits. Orientalists drawing on this literature have stressed the central position of muru'a, a virtue with strong warrior overtones in the value system of Jahiliyya beduin society.[1] Historians discussing the causes of the early Islamic conquests often speak in terms of "some outlet for the warlike energies of the Arabs,"[2] thus taking beduin fighting abilities as axiomatic and decisive. Ibn Khaldun's famous antithesis between badawa and hadara is of course based on the characterization of nomads as essentially predatory--virile, uncorrupt, and courageous, but profoundly inimical to the civilized character of sedentary life. It is this antithesis that he uses to explain the cyclical character of medieval Islamic political history.

H. Rosenfeld's article "The Social Composition of the Military in the Process of State Formation in the Arabian Desert" is one of the rare attempts to analyze in detail the military significance of Arab nomads in relation to sedentary communities.[3] This is a very interesting discussion based on material from European travelers in nineteenth-century central Arabia; unfortunately, Rosenfeld sometimes fails to follow through the implications of his own data. In general, he tends to represent the relations between pastoralists and cultivators as inherently antagonistic (an assumption I believe to be questionable), and lays great stress on the alleged military advantage of nomads over sedentaries. Thus:

> It is clear . . . that some settlements can build up their internal strength and remain relatively free of Bedouin control, can even control tribes, or be in military alliance

> with some tribes as against the towns or tribes, although in constant danger of Bedouin attack, and the cutting down of their palm-groves, the filling up of their wells, demolishing buildings, etc.
>
> But the more the settlement increases in power and wealth, the more they strive to repel or moderate the nomads' claims. However, a common situation (at least before the rise of the Saudian state) is one where the nomads hold tributary to them oases or settlements, collecting the tribute or giving settlers protection.
>
> This appears to be an ancient process. The military Bedouin "protect" the settlement from raiders, thieves, and plunderers. Essentially, they "protect" the settlers from the tribe that gives protection and from other raiders as well.[4]

A careful reading of Rosenfeld's article shows that, on the contrary, a thriving agricultural-cum-commercial center has greater resources for dominating surrounding nomadic tribes than the other way around. The most recent historical evidence from sixth-century Arabia also reveals a general pattern of nomads being dominated by sedentaries.

A Case of Direct (Military) Domination by Sedentaries over Beduin: Sixth-Century Hira

The Sassanid/Byzantine rivalry for control of trade routes passing through the Arabian peninsula during the sixth century involved the vassal Arab kingdoms of Hira and Ghassan. There is evidence of Sassanid control of sorts over Medina, at least until the middle of the sixth century, through an amil appointed by the king of Hira. Yet the effective domination of Hira (located in present-day Iraq) over the beduin never extended so far along the interior of Arabia. Its rulers had governors on the borders of the country from Iraq to Bahrayn, each governor ruling beduins under his protection who were expected to pay taxes. In relation to Hira,

> tribes could . . . be divided into three groups: (a) the independent tribes, laqah, who raided the territory of the rulers of al-Hira and were raided by them, (b) tribes who concluded pacts with the rulers of al-Hira on certain terms, and (c) tribes who pastured in the vicinity of al-Hira and were obedient to the rulers of al-Hira.[5]

The rulers of Hira drew most of their income from trade, taxes, and booty from raids against beduin. The chiefs of friendly beduin tribes were appointed as tax-collectors, as military leaders of auxiliary (beduin) forces, and as court officials. In general,

> the rulers of al-Hira could impose their sway on the tribes either by granting the chiefs benefits [such as fiefs] . . . or by force. The rulers based their power on their troops. The troops were, however, not levied from a certain tribe: there was no tribe ruling al-Hira; it was a family. The rulers of al-Hira had therefore to rely on foreign troops or on mercenary troops. Only occasionally could they use a tribal force against another tribal unit, hostile to the first.[6]

The pattern in this case is of a sedentary family of rulers drawing their wealth from agriculture, taxation, and trade, basing their major military support on mercenaries, and effectively dominating some beduin and attempting to subjugate others. The relative ability of nomad pastoralists to escape subjection to the rulers of Hira seems to have been determined in large part by the proximity of their pastures to Hira and on their need for Hira as a supply center.[7] It seems that, to some extent at least, the farther the pasture from Hira, the poorer it was.[8] Hence, an old dilemma: whether to pasture in better country and be liable to the certainty of heavy taxation, or to pasture in more remote country and be vulnerable to the possibility of drought. The greater any tribe's dependence on pastoralism as a mode of subsistence, the more acute this dilemma. Looked at another way, the more peripheral the area occupied by a given tribe (whether primarily involved in pastoralism or oasis agriculture or caravan trade), the greater its incentive to resist Hira's domination.[9] From Hira's point of view this resistance might be seen as a threat, both to the security of its subjects and of its trade routes, but there is no reason for the anthropologist to adopt the Hira viewpoint as his own, and to speak of the difficulties of restraining nomadic tribesmen when what is also involved is the difficulty of subjugating and exploiting them.

A Case of Indirect (Commercial) Domination by Sedentaries over Beduin: Sixth-Century Mecca

In the Arabian peninsula of the sixth century there were numerous sedentary communities involved in trade or agriculture--or both. How far the total beduin population of that time was involved in trade and agriculture in addition to pastoralism is not clear. According to D.F. Eickelman:

> Recent studies by R.B. Serjeant suggest that the most typical pattern in central Arabia by which a city would acquire ascendency over neighbouring tribes and regions was to form (or be selected for) a _haram_, which could constitute "a nucleus about which may be gathered an indefinite number of tribes." Several tribes (or sections of one tribe) would

> agree to recognize a given town or region as a sanctuary in which no blood could be shed, to meet there to discuss blood disputes and other serious inter-tribal matters, to allow each other to conduct trade in peace, and to arrange for the safe transit of caravans through their respective territories. To violate the rules of a haram was to risk supernatural sanctions and reprisals by other contracting tribes.[10]

Mecca, from about the middle of the century, was the most important of these sanctuaries. Its rise to power coincided with the decline of Hira, which was affected by the general political weakening of the Sassanid empire. At first the Quraysh merchants in Mecca were occupied in local commerce only: foreign traders brought goods to Mecca which the Quraysh then sold to townsmen and the surrounding tribes. Later, the Meccan merchants obtained permission from the Byzantines to bring goods directly to Syria, and made pacts (called ilafs) with tribal chiefs on the way, giving the caravans security in return for the opportunity to participate in the Syrian trade. Kister provides this account:

> Mecca, a small centre for distribution of goods for the beduin tribes in the vicinity of the city, rose to the position of an important centre for transit trade. It was the merchants of Mecca, who carried the wares to Syria, Abyssinia, al-Iraq and al-Yaman. . . . The trade based on the pacts of ilaf was a joint enterprise of the clans of Quraysh. . . . The pacts concluded with the tribes were based on the hitherto unknown principle of trade interest. It was not an alliance (hilf) with obligations of mutual help and protection. It was not an obligation to guard the caravans of Quraysh against payment, as practiced by the tribes in their relations with the caravans of al-Hira. The ilaf agreements were set up on a base of share in profit for the heads of the tribes and apparently employment of the men of the tribe as escort of the caravans.[11]

The pattern in this case is of a sedentary group of merchants basing their power on a cooperative trade enterprise involving beduins but managed by the merchants. It is primarily the general profitability of the trade, along with the religious organizations connected with the haram, that ensures the "Pax-Meccana." The Meccan merchant leaders intermarry with the families of the chiefs of the Bani Tamim, one of the most important groups of beduin tribes between Mecca and Hira. In some instances the ilaf is represented by classical sources as a tax "imposed on the tribes in order to defend Mecca from the 'wolves of the tribes,' brigands and hostile tribes."[12] Thus, under circumstances not altogether clear, the voluntary contribution by some beduin participants to a profitable commercial enterprise--"The Commonwealth of Mecca"--becomes transmuted into a compulsory tax for the defense of the capital of that enterprise.

That the Meccan merchants could accomplish such a transformation of exchange relations in the absence of a standing army is an indication both of the politico-commercial supremacy of Quraysh and of the extent of beduin dependence on trade.

In part this trade involvement was complementary to pastoralism (e.g., the selling of animals) and in part an alternative to it (e.g., the provision of animal transport or service as paid militiamen or full-time commercial activity), but in what proportions we do not know. The problem of "surplus men" available for activities other than full-time pastoralism is connected with the manner of such trade involvement--and more generally with the kinds of property and work arrangements obtaining in a pastoral society. To talk of surplus men in the context of pastoralism is to talk of unequal access to animal resources: surplus men are either poor men who have an insufficient number of animals to be pastoralists and must therefore look elsewhere for their livelihood, or they are rich men who have so many animals that they need not themselves labor for their livelihood. Both kinds of men may turn to military activity--as a source of livelihood in the one case, as a means of reinforcing power in the other. In the structure of domination represented by the Commonwealth of Mecca, the military element appears as a minor feature when compared with Hira, but this seems to have less to do with the nomadic-sedentary antithesis than with the character of property distribution and with modes of exploitation.

A Case of Beduins Conquering an Empire: The Early Islamic Conquests

Describing the early conquests of Islam in the seventh century, a standard history of the Arabs states: "Not fanaticism but economic necessity drove the Bedouin hordes, and most of the armies of conquest were recruited from the Bedouins, beyond the confines of their arid abode to the fair land of the north."[13] Whatever the motive for these conquests may have been, a question which seems to have received comparatively little attention from historians is the extent to which these "beduin hordes" were pastoral nomads, and how their previous mode of livelihood fitted into the context of a conquering army.

A recent work has unravelled some of the details concerning the constitution of the Arab armies.[14] The armies consisted both of _ahl al-qura_ (sedentary tribes) and of _ahl al-wabar_ (nomadic tribes), but it is not clear how many of the latter had previously been primarily dependent on pastoralism. There is no evidence that the Arab armies were organized into units of pastoralists or cultivators, or that in the parceling out of conquered lands the former were given pasture land and the latter agricultural land. Many soldiers received cultivable land which they farmed in either the agricultural sense or the tax sense. Others received stipends of cash, or foodstuffs and clothing, from the appropriate treasury. All of this suggests that at the time of the conquests the ahl al-wabar were not dependent on animals as their primary source of livelihood. Certainly the beduin armies which inhabited such garrison towns as Kufah and Fustat--armies indispensable to the expanding Islamic order--had more in common with mercenaries than with pastoralists, even though they may have owned many animals.

Pastoralists may help to conquer new territory, but they cannot constitute a regular state army and remain pastoralists. There is even reason to doubt that the major part of the early Arabian army was pastoralist at the time of the first conquests. The ridda (civil war) campaigns across the length and breadth of the Arabian peninsula immediately after the death of the Prophet Muhammad seriously disrupted the network of trade on which so many had depended (a point stressed by Shaban), and probably led to the destruction of considerable numbers of animals (thus depriving pastoralists of their primary means of subsistence). The result of this wholesale elimination of their source of livelihood may well have "proletarianized" a large proportion of the beduin into a pool of propertyless men who could be effectively mobilized into a conquering army.

A Case of Beduins Ravaging an Empire: The Bani Hilal in Eleventh-Century North Africa

According to the view accepted since the time of Ibn Khaldun, one of the great events of medieval Islamic history was the destruction by the Bani Hilal pastoralists of the agricultural prosperity of the Maghreb. This is often cited as a classic example of the profound conflict between militant pastoralism and agricultural civilization. But in the last few years a radical reevaluation of this period has begun--first in J. Poncet, "Le myth de la catastrophe hilalienne,"[15] and then in C. Cahen, "Quelques mots sur les Hilaliens et le nomadisme."[16]

Poncet in effect reverses the traditional account by arguing that the political and economic decline of the Maghreb preceded and facilitated the Hilalian invasions: the shifting of the Fatimid caliphate from Ifriqiya (eastern Maghreb) to Egypt in the third quarter of the tenth century transformed Ifriqiya from the center of a powerful empire into a peripheral area. Coincident with this shift, the maritime trade routes were beginning to be diverted from Ifriqiya to Sicily and the rising ports of coastal Italy, which now had strong direct ties with Egypt. Ifriqiya, under the vassal Berber dynasty of the Zaridis, was torn by internal political struggles which not only weakened the military apparatus of the state but also contributed to the destruction of agriculture. It was during these internal struggles that the Zaridi ruler broke officially with the Fatimids. Apparently when the Hilalians arrived from Egypt (at the instigation of the Fatimids), they found that the local leaders preferred to come to an understanding with the Hilalian pastoralists rather than remain submissive to the Zaridis.

Cahen finds this reinterpretation convincing, and adds some interesting general observations:

> There is a wider problem than the invasion of the Hilalians. If one looks at the whole Muslim world in the tenth and eleventh centuries, it is clear that one is witnessing a general process of beduinization in the political world. The Arab-Asiatic Near East, on the ruins of the Abbasid caliphate, whose disintegration owes nothing to beduinism, saw the birth of the great Arab semi-beduin principality of the Hamdanids (upper Mesopotamia and upper Syria), itself replaced a century later by the purely beduin local dynasties of the 'Uqaylids, Mirdasids, Mazyadites, etc. To the northeast, in somewhat comparable Kurdish conditions, other principalities were born. In Egypt itself, the role of the "Arabs" was growing. From outside, all this was to be choked off by the Turks, but they were themselves semi-nomadic. The formation of Hilalian power, seen against this background, is thus only one case--perhaps important, but not unique--of a general phenomenon which cannot be explained by purely special factors. It is difficult for us to say whether the conquest of power by princes from a beduin milieu was sometimes or always accompanied by a development of beduinism. [Thus] the political rise of the beduins could be due simply to a collapse of other elements of power in states where they already lived, which is not to say that they played no part whatever in it. In the case of the Abbasid caliphate, there was anarchy in the heart of the professional army, which gave relative strength to those elements of the population with warlike intentions, and regional emancipation, which gave increased influence to one or another social element according to who was dominant in the area in question without their being dominated in turn by officials of the central state, etc. Whatever the case, as often happens in history, there is room for a comparative study of the beduin phenomena in all the Muslim world (if not beyond it), particularly in the heart of the Middle Ages.[17]

Cahen senses, but does not make quite explicit, the important distinction between beduinism as a form of life and beduinism as a form of claimed descent.

Thus the possibility arises of seeing the destruction of irrigation and the simultaneous "beduinization" (pastoralization) of local economies as consequences of historical processes in which the military force used by the beduins is of minor importance. Apart from the collapse of internal military security within the state and of the emergence of autonomous political regions, long-term economic factors may make for a retreat of the agricultural frontier between the desert and the sown. It is worth remembering that prior to the modern era with its unique incentives and pressures (demographic, technological, and economic) for promoting agriculture, marginal cultivated land might be abandoned to pastoralists quite independently of any military threat from the latter--because of population shortage, the declining value of certain agricultural products, or the desire to escape from an extortionate government.

But even where the pastoralist advance is locally resisted, it is always worth inquiring into the wider historical circumstances which make for the strength or weakness of centralized states along whose borders the nomads are located. Although to the Zaridi rulers the incoming Hilalian pastoralists may have appeared in the guise of a *sui generis* nomadic scourge, to the Fatimids they were merely a useful political instrument which could be directed against the dissident vassal dynasty in Ifriqiya.

A Case of Beduins Resisting a Modern Colonial Empire: The Italians in Cyrenaica

The power of agricultural-based states of the pre-modern Islamic world was vitally affected by disasters of drought and epidemic, by the diversion of maritime and caravan trade routes, and by the destruction wrought by internal military struggles. In between the cyclical rise and decline of stable, powerful governments, pastoralists might in favorable conditions generate an effective military force--for defense or offense--in relation to a given group of sedentaries. But with the rise of industrial capitalism, the existence of international systems of finance and sophisticated technology have combined to give central governments a stability which is invulnerable to any military force that beduins alone might muster or support. Neither their proverbial ease of mobility nor their occupation of marginal lands has much military significance when they face opponents having armored cars, airplanes, and unlimited supplies of men and material.

Evans-Pritchard's well-known account of the Cyrenaican beduin resistance (organized and led by the Sanusi order) to Italian colonization indicates, roughly speaking, three military phases in the war: first, the Italians attempted to subdue the beduins through the use of regular army units; second, they made greater use of airplanes and small motorized units; third, they employed the strategy of massive concentration camps:

> Their experience in the barqa taught the Italians afresh the lesson of 1911 to 1915, that against Bedouin unwieldy columns advancing without concealment in a direct line on definite and fixed objectives could lead to little more than skirmishes, for the enemy was too wise to become involved in decisive action and mobile enough to avoid it; so they adopted the new tactics of making surprise raids by mechanised units on the Bedouin encampments, slaughtering man and beast indiscriminately, and destroying the grain stores. In these raids, on what in a noncolonial war would be regarded as the civilian population, the purpose was to kill as many of the Bedouin as possible, striking terror into the hearts of the shepherd folk of Cyrenaica. When the rains came and mechanised transport could no longer be used, the camps were bombed and machine-gunned from the air. The Bedouin suffered greatly from this persistent strafing, the Italian estimate of their losses--I must repeat that Italian figures are highly suspect--from 6 March to 3 September 1923 being 800 killed, 230 captured, and 1,000 wounded, besides about 700 camels and 22,000 sheep killed or confiscated.[18]

And in the later phase of the resistance:

> Graziani was determined to wrest the initiative from the guerrillas. He reorganized his forces for the last round in the "guerra senza quartiere" into small mobile patrols to keep the whole of the forest country under surveillance and to attack the enemy wherever they met him, giving him no rest. To prevent the guerrillas from obtaining supplies and reinforcements from the civilian population he disarmed the tribesmen, confiscating from them thousands of rifles and millions of rounds of ammunition, and made possession of arms a capital offence. He instituted the "tribunale volante," a military court flown from point to point to try, and execute, all who had dealings of any kind with the guerrillas. He reduced the Libyan units by more than two-thirds, with the intention of disbanding them altogether later. In the meanwhile he distributed among the 750 Libyans retained in service rifles of a different calibre from rifles in Patriot hands to prevent leakage of ammunition. At the same time he closed the Sanusiya lodges, confiscated their estates, and exiled their Shaikhs to the Island of Istica. He also much improved the communications of the colony, thereby easing his supply problem and economizing man-power.
>
> It may be doubted whether all these measures would have been effective if he had not also started his immense concentration camps for the entire tribal population of Cyrenaica, about whose feelings the General had no illusions. In taking

this step the Italians were doing no more than others had done before them and have done after them, for an army fighting guerrillas is fighting an entire population. The first concentration camps of January 1930 were found to be too near the area of military operations, for the prisoners, in spite of close surveillance, still managed to supply the guerrillas with some of their requirements; so most of the Bedouin were removed to the barqa al-baida and the Sirtica. In this bleak country were herded in the smallest camps possible 80,000 men, women and children, and 600,000 beasts in the summer of 1930. Hunger, disease, and broken hearts took a heavy toll of the imprisoned population. Bedouin die in a cage. Loss of livestock was also great, for the beasts had insufficient grazing near the camps on which to support life, and the herds, already decimated in the fighting, were almost wiped out by the camps.

The guerrillas thus found themselves cut off from local sources of supply and forced more and more to rely on Egypt for the bare necessities of life and of war. For years a considerable part of their supplies had come from there, paid for by Bedouin produce, money raised by customs charges, and funds collected throughout the Arab and Muslim world. Supplies came through the port of al-Sallum, and the Egyptian Frontiers Administration must have closed its eyes to supplies going into Cyrenaica as tightly as to refugees going out of it. The Marmarica had been declared by the Italians a military zone, its people being removed to concentration camps, and the closed frontier was patrolled by armoured cars and planes with instructions to destroy any caravans they spotted, but, in spite of these precautions, supplies continued to reach the Patriots. Graziani therefore decided to run a line of barbed-wire entanglements from the sea to Jaghbub and into the dunes to the south of it, a distance of over 300 km. The work was completed early in September 1931 and control along the wire was operated through fortified posts, a telephone system, and aviation camps.[19]

Thus even as a support base for guerrilla activity, pastoralists are more vulnerable than peasants for the simple reason that their means of subsistence can more easily be destroyed. The days of Hira, when pastoralists could successfully resist or even raid an established power, are over.

Concluding Remarks

Military force is merely one element in the realm of power relations which can be employed to impose, or resist, a structure of domination--to make incursions into another's privileged domain or to resist such incursions. The relative abilities of groups to use military force effectively do not depend directly on the distinction between nomadic and sedentary life--i.e., between being in movement and being stationary--as such. Different kinds of military objectives call for different logistical solutions (e.g., a medieval robber baron controlling a mountain pass, a revolutionary guerrilla band, a colonial army of occupation, the invading forces of continental powers at war). It makes little sense to generalize about the military advantage of nomadic mobility over sedentary immobility as such.

Historically, the military potentialities of some Middle Eastern pastoralists have been somewhat greater than those of nonpastoralists in certain irregular encounters--for example, in escaping central government forces, in disrupting caravan trade routes, or in carrying out sudden raids against outlying agricultural settlements. That is to say, pastoralists have been more successful at resisting than imposing structures of domination; those who engage in animal husbandry as their basic means of livelihood do not have the capacity to establish a permanent military advantage over cultivators on any significant scale. Whenever such an advantage has become institutionalized, an important structural development has taken place in which the terms of the initial opposition (between nomad pastoralist and sedentary cultivator) has been radically transformed (into ruler and ruled).

In the long run, the relative ability of groups to impose or resist domination depends on their access to crucial assets. The basic opposition, therefore, is not one between nomads and sedentaries, but between those who engage in the production of surplus resources and those who have control of such surplus. Another way of making this point is to say that the rulers of agricultural states are not to be grouped with the producers of agricultural wealth, any more than town-based rulers of "beduin" origin (such as both Cahen and Rosenfeld refer to) are to be classed as nomadic tribesmen--except ideologically. This is especially important in the historic Middle East where pastoral, agricultural, and trade activities are interdependent parts of a single economic system, where different elements of the exploitable population are mobilized at different levels to support the power structure, and where--in consequence--popular rebellions have often involved the temporary alliance of peasants and pastoralists.[20]

Once we take as our point of departure the analytic distinction between exploiters and exploited, the question of the relative military advantage of beduins can move from considerations of morale and logistics to a discussion of the ways in which surplus resources are historically accumulated, controlled, and deployed in order to impose, maintain, or resist structures of domination.

In this context we might be tempted to argue as follows: A "pure" pastoral productive system has a greater natural rate of growth than a "pure" agricultural one (animals reproduce themselves, fields do not); so, if unchecked, a "pure" pastoral system can generate larger surpluses than a pure agricultural system; therefore, over a period of time, the former can give rise to a more formidable military power than the latter. It is this kind of economic determinism which largely explains the frequency of nomadic conquests in the historic Middle East. (See Fredrik Barth's contribution to this volume, pp. 11-21).

However attractive such an argument might seem, I think it would be mistaken for two reasons. First, it is misleading to isolate, even conceptually, systems of production from systems of power. The household head who has regular control of family work and subsistence, the ruler who taxes his pastoral subjects in order to finance his administration, armed raiders who plunder vulnerable populations or destroy their means of livelihood or push them onto marginal territory, modern colonists who forcibly occupy and cultivate land once used by subsistence peasants and pastoralists--these are all instances of the intrinsic connection between the exercise of coercive power and modes of generating surpluses. The different systems of production do not operate in a power vacuum. A basic fact about surplus production is the relatively easier exploitability of cultivating populations. And because in general agricultural populations are more easily exploitable, the rate of accumulation of surplus resources at the service of power is always greater for an agricultural than for a pastoral productive system.

The second reason is that agriculture-based and trade-based states have been the norm for the historic Middle East. The exceptional weakness of such states sometimes permitted beduins to capture the controlling centers. When this happened, the producers of animal wealth (or some of them) became the controllers of agricultural production; this was the point at which "beduin" military capability became really formidable. Yet it did so only by abandoning its power base in pastoralism. This should be emphasized, for the reverse (i.e., the voluntary shifting of the power base from agriculture to pastoralism) seems never to have occurred. A final historical point: a weak state was vulnerable to elements other than nomads, and in fact the seizure of state power by dissidents or adventurers occurred far more often than seizure by nomads.

Footnotes

[1] See, for example, I. Goldziher, Muslim Studies, Vol. I (London, 1967), ch. 1.

[2] W.M. Watt, Muhammad at Medina (Oxford, 1956), p. 105.

[3]H. Rosenfeld, "The Social Composition of the Military in the Process of State Formation in the Arabian Desert," Journal of the Royal Anthropological Institute, Vol. 95, 1965.

[4]Ibid., p. 78. In reproducing these excerpts from Rosenfeld I have omitted the quotation marks and references which appear in the original text.

[5]M.J. Kister, "Al-Hira," Arabica, Vol. XV, 1968, p. 153.

[6]Ibid., p. 165.

[7]See ibid., p. 168.

[8]See ibid., pp. 151-52, 154.

[9]See ibid., p. 162, for incidents relating to the attempted refusal of beduins to pay Hira tax.

[10]D.F. Eickelman, "Musaylima," Journal of the Economic and Social History of the Orient, Vol. X, 1967, p. 25.

[11]M.J. Kister, "Mecca and Tamim," Journal of the Economic and Social History of the Orient, Vol. VIII, 1965, p. 120.

[12]Ibid., p. 143.

[13]P.K. Hitti, History of the Arabs (London, 1964), p. 144.

[14]M.A. Shaban, Islamic History: A.D. 600-750 (A.H. 132); A New Interpretation (Cambridge, 1971).

[15]J. Poncet, "Le myth de la catastrophe hilalienne," Annales: Economie, Sociétés, Civilisations, Vol. XXII, 1967.

[16]C. Cahen, "Quelques mots sur les Hilaliens et le nomadisme," Journal of the Economic and Social History of the Orient, Vol. XI, 1968.

[17]Ibid., p. 132.

[18]E.E. Evans-Pritchard, The Sanusi of Cyrenaica (Oxford, 1949), p. 175.

[19]Ibid., pp. 188-89.

[20]See, for example, A.N. Poliak, "Les Révoltes populaires en Egypte à l'époque de Mamelouks et leurs causes économiques," Revue des Etudes Islamiques, Vol. VIII, 1934.

TRIBAL AND SEDENTARY ELITES: A BRIDGE BETWEEN TWO COMMUNITIES

Abdel Ghaffar M. Ahmed

In treating nomad-sedentary relationships, much attention has been paid to the difficulties of coexistence of such populations and their integration on the social level within the boundaries of one environment, as well as the stereotyping of their relationships on the abstract level. It is only within the frame of a few of these studies that an adequate explanation of the ongoing processes of interaction between these communities on the basis of their value systems can be seen.[1] This seems to result from a reluctance to apply explanatory models to such situations of interaction, and to follow the development of different processes to their logical outcome. We should be able to design such "models" so that they can "explain how the observable frequency patterns, or regularities, are generated. . . . [They] should mirror actual, empirical processes which can be identified in the reality which is being analysed,"[2] so that the adequacy of these models can be tested through comparisons.

In this paper I shall look at the relationships between nomads and sedentary population in one region--namely, the Funj area of the southern part of the Gezira between the Blue and the White Niles in the Sudan. To be more specific, I shall examine the relationships between one nomadic ethnic group and the sedentary population on the banks of the Blue Nile sharing the same Rural Council (Abu Hugar). This relationship can best be understood if one focuses on its transactional aspects, whether in the field of politics or domestic economy, which are the subject of everyday interaction. These are transactions of a special character. They are not only between two parties, but a third party is also involved. This approach utilizes the concept of "elites," and explains their role as middlemen in certain situations. The relations between the "elites" and the "masses" can be viewed within the boundaries of their ethnic groups except when ethnic boundaries are crossed. In a situation where a person identifies another as a member of his own ethnic group, it is assumed that they share the same cultural standards and have agreed on the "rules of the game" they are playing. To categorize someone as a member of a different ethnic group implies a recognition of a limitation on shared understanding; consequently, interaction is restricted primarily to sectors of activities where common understanding is assumed. The "elite" may not often take the role of middlemen within their ethnic groups, but in many societies the moment transactions cross ethnic boundaries, the "elite's" role as middlemen becomes indispensable. This is because the assumed common understanding noted above is now put to the test, and an individual from the mass will not dare to take the risk of entering into a direct transaction with a person from another ethnic group. The ability of the elite in the management and conversion of values is needed. The elites of the different groups in such an interaction are playing a game, one of the rules of which is to keep some information from the masses. The elites have their own interests which they serve before anything else. Different elites of different ethnic groups who happen to be utilizing the same ecological niche have to cooperate and/or compete when they come into contact to enforce their idea of the value of the items transacted. Sometimes they might ally and share the rewards which are the outcome, and hide information from the masses on both sides. In most cases they are the entrepreneurs in their communities.

The nomad-sedentary relationship is not one of hostility, as some planners and administrators maintain. The studies noted above emphasize its complementary or symbiotic nature. I am here drawing attention to specific interactions which are of great importance to an understanding of nomad-sedentary relationships. I am trying to emphasize the role of the elites as key figures in such situations. They are the bridge that brings these communities together. It is only through our ability to grasp their role as value managers that we can understand the relationships between nomads and sedentary populations in most places.

The Region

The Funj area lies roughly between lat. 13'40° and 9'30° N. The Blue and the White Niles can be regarded as the eastern and western boundaries. The northern limit is the Sennar-Kosti railway line, and the southern limit is set by the Machare marshes, the Ethiopian highlands, and the Sudan-Ethiopian international boundary. The whole area is a clay plain with very small patches of sand in the north. The largest hill mass in the area is the Ingessana hills, which rise to over 300 meters; there are a few other isolated hills of less height.

Climatically the area is what is known as low rain woodland savannah. The rainfall is heavier toward the south. It ranges between 400 mm. at the northern limit and above 700 mm. at the southern boundary, falling mainly between the end of April and the end of October. The rain usually starts earlier and stops later in the south than in the north.

With reference to vegetation, the area can be divided into four types. Thornland alternates with grass areas in the north. Further south, Acacia seyal balanites savannah alternates with grass areas, and then savannah woodland appears, with the Ingessana hills and the hill catena in the middle.

The Elites

Every society has its elites. Of the number of types of elites who come under the broad definition given by the classical theorists of elites--Mosca and Pareto--my concern is with those who are referred to by Mills as the "power elite." They are defined "in terms of the means of power--as those who occupy the command posts."[3] My emphasis is mainly on political and economic fields, "but the separation of these two fields is often very arbitrary. The economic relations are relations of power and are thus essentially political, forming part of the political order of the society."[4] Nadel gives a definition of the elite which is useful here. He defines it as a segment in a society which "can claim a position of superiority and hence a corresponding measure of influence over the fate of the community." In this context an elite may be one of three basic types: "A group whose superiority rests on especial acquired skills and talent; a group whose superiority is traditional and quite unspecialized [or] a group constituting a reservoir of skills and talents of all kinds."[5]

The ruling family of Abu Rūf of the Rufāᶜa al-Hoi tribe represent what I refer to as a tribal elite.[6] With the use of patrilineal descent ideology, they legitimize their claims for positions of authority in the tribe, which were institutionalized during the period of Anglo-Egyptian rule in the Sudan and continued after independence was obtained. Through these positions they have command over the important economic resources in the area and hence exert major influence on the fate of the community, being the main decision-making body in situations where the interest of the whole tribe is involved. Among the sedentary populations the situation is rather different, and in many cases political power is acquired by reversing this pattern. Through the ability to utilize the economic resources available, one acquires economic power, which is subsequently converted into political power, giving access to more economic resources.

Among the sedentary populations I distinguish two types of elites. One is the "religious elite," and the other is the elite basing their claim on political or economic resources only. The religious elite were at one time predominant among the sedentary population, and exercised some influence on the nomads as well during the early Mahdist revolution. Later this section of the elite declined, and the merchants who are the present elite rose in their place. The religious elite had both religious and economic power, which they transformed into political power through playing the role of mediators. The merchant elite sprang up mainly as a dominant economic power and converted that power to political use.

In Nadel's discussion of elites, he states that they "must have some degree of corporateness, group character, and exclusiveness. There must be barriers of admission."[7] These could be seen as characteristics of the tribal elite, but they would then be pictured as an extreme group raised high above the rest of the mass who are part of the political arena. In reality this is not the case. The Abu Rūf family leaders, who are less than thirty office-holders, are closely connected with the masses through a large group of sub-elite occupying intermediary power positions--i.e., camp leaders (*shaykhs* of *farigs*).

The sedentary elite lack the high degree of corporateness that the tribal elite have. The social situation is one in which different ethnic groups interact freely, and recruitment on the basis of ethnicity and descent is not of great significance in the formation of the sedentary elite group. Admission is based on skill, talent, and ability to act as an entrepreneur. The corporateness the elite acquire is on the basis of common interests. Their number is small in each village, and they reach general agreements on the sharing of benefits. They also set limits as to how far internal competition can continue without danger of reducing the benefits. In this respect admission can be difficult if the already existing group does not want to allow room for more competitors. The size of this elite is relatively large compared to the tribal elite, especially after the rapid growth of the al-Mazmum and al-Garabein market centers due to the establishment of the Mechanical Crop Production Schemes.

The Rufā^{c}a al-Hoi Nomads

The Rufā^{c}a al-Hoi is an Arabic-speaking Muslim nomadic group whose arrival in its present habitat can be dated back to the fourteenth century.[8] It consists of two large sections--the Bani Hassan and the Bani Husayn--and a third relatively smaller one--the Shibaylāt. The total population of the group is more than 26,000.[9] They are divided into two parts on the basis of their annual migrations. The northern *badiya*, who spend the dry season on the banks of the Blue Nile between Abu Hugar and al-Roseires, include approximately one-third of the total population. The southern badiya, who spend the dry season on the *khors* Tombak, Ahmar, Yabus, and the fringes of the Machare marshes, make up the other two-thirds. Both badiyas spend the wet season west of al-Mazmum and al-Dali, and some go as far as Jebel Moya. They compete with other nomadic groups in the area such as the Kinānā, the White Nile Baggara tribes, the Ingessana, and the pastoral Fulani, who moved into the area recently. Sedentary people from various ethnic groups are settled in the area either on the banks of the Blue and White Niles or in villages on the plains.

The Rufāᶜa al-Hoi nomads keep camels, cattle, sheep, and goats. The southern badiya keep a small number of camels for carrying the household baggage, since they move in an area climatically unfavorable for camels. The southern badiya of the Rufāᶜa al-Hoi maintain larger herds of cattle and sheep than the northern badiya. It is almost impossible to give any estimate of the animal population of the area, since the animal records kept in the rural council (Abu Hugar) are considered unreliable by the administrators themselves.

The basic unit in the Rufāᶜa al-Hoi nomadic organization is the household, since it is the production and consumption unit as well as the base for domestic authority and of great political significance at the camp level.[10] The household occupies a tent made of either wool mats, straw mats, or cloth, and is composed of the household head, his wife and young children and grown-up daughters. In cases of polygamy, each wife has her own tent, with the household head dividing his time between the two or more households. Some households may have dependents attached to them, such as an old father and mother or a divorced sister. In a few cases, a newly married daughter who has not yet moved to her husband's camp may have her own tent pitched beside that of her mother, but usually this is done only when the husband is visiting her, and the tent is removed when he goes to join his herding unit. Men spend all the day time (when they have nothing or little to do) in the _khalwa_,[11] and unmarried men spend the night there.

Consistent with the patrilineal descent ideology, which is very strong among the Rufāᶜa al-Hoi, camp clusters emerge consisting of closely connected households. A camp cluster may consist of 10 to 15 households, depending on the water and grazing conditions in the area. The term _farig_ can be used to refer to such a cluster, but usually it refers to a number of these clusters (5-6) which are administratively organized under one leader (_shaykh_). The camp cluster forms the herding unit of the Rufāᶜa al-Hoi, and its population ranges between 300 and 400 persons. The total number of camps making up the Rufāᶜa al-Hoi tribe is 71.

In reality the composition of the camp cluster (as distinguished from the administratively recognized camp) does not conform with the accepted patrilineal descent ideology. There are many individuals and households attached to one cluster who trace their genealogies to different clusters or sometimes even to different tribes. What makes them join such a cluster is a matter of choice. Some come as herders, marry, and stay, or some bring their families with them and find it profitable to stay.

The reputation and the generosity of the senior man or men is of great importance in attracting such individuals.

In the Rufāᶜa al-Hoi economy, the nomads strive for the best utilization of all the resources their environment provides.[12] They have a subsistence economy which is based on three kinds of assets. Traditionally their major assets have been camels, cattle, or sheep, together with a few goats, and grazing rights, but recently they have developed an interest in gum tapping as a source of cash income.

The Camp Leaders as a Sub-Elite

The shaykhs of farigs represent what I referred to earlier as the sub-elite in the tribal structure. Apart from the descent ideology, the shaykhs are the only link between the elite and the masses. They hold intermediary positions in the tribal organization which are semi-hereditary. When the shaykh of a farig dies, one of his sons is usually chosen by the elders of the farig to take his place. This choice has to be confirmed by the Abu Rūf leader of the tribe before the council administrators recognize it, however. The shaykh's duties include the collection of taxes, out of which he gets a certain percentage, settling internal disputes, and representing the camp to the tribal leader. The only situation in which he represents the camp to the outside world is where compensation committees are set up to evaluate damage made by his farig's herds to the sedentary population's crops. This does not happen very often because such disputes are usually taken to the tribal leaders or the umdas courts.

The shaykh's building of political support within and outside the boundaries of the camp depends on his charismatic attributes as well as his economic ability. The degree of hospitality he can show is a major factor in building his political career because it attracts followers from even outside the tribe. With a large number of followers supporting him, he can emerge as a dominant figure among the sub-elite and get close to the elite. The elite might consult him on issues involving the general interest of the tribe, and in many cases give him access to the resources monopolized by the leading elite--i.e., gum gardens--or consult him when taxes are estimated.

Yet the sub-game played by the sub-elite is under the total control of the leading elite. The relationship between these two groups is not always a smooth one. The sub-elite is reminded continually of the part they have to play within the rules stated by the elite. Threats of dismissal of camp leaders through accusations of embezzling taxes or by division of a section between rivals are often used.

The Tribal Elite

Through the history of the Rufāᶜa al-Hoi tribe, one family has remained the leading family both in the fields of politics and economics. This is the Abu Rūf family, to whose great ancestors the whole section of the Bani Hassan is related, while the Bani Husayn and the Shibaylāt maintain that their early ancestors were brothers of Abu Rūf. According to oral tradition, they led the tribe to its present habitat and established its dominance by defeating those who were then occupying the area. Sometimes the name Abu Rūf is used to mean the whole Rufāᶜa al-Hoi group or only one large section of it (i.e., Bani Hassan). James Bruce used Abu Rūf to refer to the nomads of the Gezira who refused to pay dues to the Funj kings.[13] Other travelers have referred to the Abu Rūf leaders, but have given no mention of the rest of the tribe.[14] When the Khalifa Abdallahi sent his soldiers against the Abu Rūf leaders in 1887, he destroyed all the Bani Hassan section.[15] At the beginning of the Anglo-Egyptian Condominium, administrators used the names Rufāᶜa al-Hoi and Abu Rūf to mean the same section, in contrast to the Bani Husayn, which they kept separate.

All this suggests that the status of the Abu Rūf as a leading group of the Rufāᶜa al-Hoi is not a new feature in the history of the area that can be attributed to external influence after 1900. It is not only the institutionalization of power positions that has made the rest of the tribe, now referred to as Rufāᶜa al-Hoi, accept their leadership. They have traditionally been seen as the representatives of the tribe to the government and the rest of the outside world.

All three sections of the Rufāᶜa al-Hoi suffered in one way or another from the Mahdiya. Elsewhere I have discussed in detail the politics of the Rufāᶜa al-Hoi nazirate[16] and the role of the sedentary population in it.[17] Here I will review briefly part of that discussion.

After the Reoccupation, the two leading families of the two major sections--the Abu Rūf family of Bani Hassan and the Abd al Tam family of Bani Husayn--consolidated and regained the political power they had lost during the Mahdiya. They used the authority given to them by the Condominium government not only to secure their power positions, but also to destroy those who had opposed them during the Mahdiya. This was sometimes done openly and at other times by covert means. They dominated the sedentary population in the area as well. The Abu Rūf family took over the offices that had been allotted to the sedentary, and allowed them only a minor role in nazirate politics. It is only since 1964 that the sedentary population has reemerged as a significant body in the politics of the area.

An important thing to note about the Abu Rūf family is that its members have been settled (i.e., stationary) since the early days of the Condominium rule. They have monopolized all the power positions in their area, whether among the nomads or the sedentary population. Their settlement is attributed to the fact that their wealth in animals was confiscated by the Khalifa Abdallahi in 1887. When their first nazir was appointed in 1900, they had only a few animals, which did not provide the minimum required capital for a nomadic life; therefore, they sent the animals off with closely related camp leaders. Together with the Bani Husayn leaders, they were given authority over the distribution of gum gardens and allowed to take a certain amount of money from that source. With this income and the percentage they got from the taxes they collected, they achieved a good economic position within their tribe in a short time. Being settled, they took advantage of their situation of being close to the government authorities and made contacts with officials that enabled them to consolidate their power as against their rivals--the Bani Husayn and the rest of the tribe. Education was one of their assets, and eventually they were able to concentrate all official jobs within the family. Even to jobs such as local police they appointed their dependents and slaves, and thereby managed to constitute themselves as an exclusive power group.

The sub-elite were very important to them as their link with the masses, and the multiplication of the number of sub-elite in the early 1950's became an important aspect of nazirate politics. With the establishment of the Rural Council in 1953, the Abu Rūf family felt that it was important to multiply the number of camp leaders of their section so that in any election on such a level it would not be possible for their rivals (the Bani Husayn) and the sedentary people to outvote them. This policy was successful on two levels: it gave them (1) numerical superiority over their rivals and (2) control over their own sub-elite through threats of splitting camps and creating new units.

From their position as settled leaders of nomads, it can be seen that the Abu Rūf are involved in two different games requiring different strategies in manipulating the resources related to each. The game in which the individual household unit, the sub-elite, and the elite (being related through descent ideology, ecological situation, similar economic resources, and a channel of authority) are involved can be summed up in the term "tribal politics." This is a game concerning the resources which are available to the Rufā^{c}a al-Hoi tribesmen. The general knowledge that the Abu Rūf elite have acquired through their contact with the sedentary population and government officials qualifies them to represent the interests of the tribe in the council arena. They have the support of the masses. To play the role demanded of them by the nomadic population, the Abu Rūf elite have to take part in one or more sub-games where the resources from the nomads' sphere must be transformed strategically into other forms so that they can be used effectively in the new situation. The tribe has to present a solid front no matter how much conflict there is between rivals within the tribe.

The game played between the Abu Rūf and the sedentary elites is over the rewards emerging from the decisions made in the council arena. These involve benefits arising from development projects in the area, distribution of land for Mechanized Crop Production Schemes, and control over the different decision-making committees appointed by the council. Through such benefits the Abu Rūf can consolidate their power within the boundaries of the tribe and maintain their superior position.

Sedentary Population

During their seasonal migration the Rufāᶜa al-Hoi come into contact with some of the sedentary populations of the area. Some of these people practice agriculture, cultivating various crops both for subsistence and marketing, and keep a few animals. Those on the banks of the Blue Nile either own small pieces of land or work as tenants on pump schemes owned by absentee landlords who live in towns such as Singa and Sennar. Those who are in the villages in the northern parts of the plains either work in the Mechanical Crop Production Schemes or cultivate dura and sesame in the wet season (*kharief*) and tap gum in the dry season. Those in the southern part of the plains cultivate in kharief also, but on such a small scale that it is only enough for subsistence, with perhaps a small margin of profit (in good years) which is exchanged for material goods in village shops. Their modes of living and cultural traits vary considerably from those of the nomads.

The major economic resource of the majority of the sedentary people is land. Private ownership of land in the area on the banks of the Blue Nile north of latitude 10° N. can be traced back to the Funj Sultanate (1504-1821). Most of the land was given to senior members of the sultan's court, such as *wazīrs* (ministers), *meks* (governors), *muqaddams* (generals), *gadis* (judges), and *walis* (religious leaders). The plains remained communally held by the nomad groups.

The religious leaders settled with their followers on the lands granted to them by the sultans, while the other categories of leaders became overlords to tenants with whom they had no direct contact and no personal ties. They had agents to manage their estates and collect dues for them while they remained in Sennar.

The Turkish administration (1821-1883) made land grants to influential persons either as special favors or as a way of bringing as much land as possible under cultivation. During the Mahdist rule (1885-1898) the ownership of vast territories was transferred from disloyal individuals or groups to loyal ones. Large areas of cultivated land turned to waste after the occupants had been massacred or forced to migrate. But with the fall of the Mahdist regime, parts of the lands reverted to the original holders who had survived. The Anglo-Egyptian Condominium established in 1899 was interested in protecting the tenants, especially in the Singa area. By 1905 it was determined that no land was to be sold without the approval of the province governor.[18]

In dealing with the sedentary elite in this area, I will limit my discussion to those who live within the boundaries of the Rufāᶜa al-Hoi nazirate of the Abu Hugar council. The sedentary population under the administration of this nazirate is more than 28,000. The majority live in villages on the banks of the Blue Nile between the area slightly north of Abu Hugar and south of Wad al Nayil. The rest are settled in villages scattered on the plains west of the Blue Nile.

The sedentary population of the Rufāᶜa al-Hoi are generally referred to by the term "Fellata," of whom the majority came to the area in the early days of the Condominium. There is also a large number of western Sudanese, mainly Tunjur, Fur, Zaghawa, Hamar, and Bani Halba, who were part of the Mahdist army and moved south after the battle of Omdurman (1898). There are northern Sudanese groups in the area (such as Ja'aliyin) from whom the majority of the present elite came. There are two villages on the bank of the Blue Nile of settled Rufāᶜa al-Hoi from the Shibaylāt section. On the plain there are at least three villages whose population is predominantly Rufāᶜa al-Hoi, who recently settled because of their inability to maintain a nomadic mode of life. The rest of the villages on the plains are a mixture of the various ethnic groups cited.

At the village level there is a great diversity of forms of social organization and culture. Many of the villages are small and compact. They are essentially similar in their physical aspects, but highly diversified with respect to their ethnic composition, ranging from exclusively West African settlers to communities where all the ethnic groups noted above are represented. In household organization the range is wide. Extended families of large numbers live side by side with incomplete families (e.g., widow(er) and child, single man and mother). In terms of access to the major economic resource--land--the range is from free landowners to tenants working for absentee landowners. There is considerable variation in village populations, from a minimum of one thousand to a maximum of several thousand.

The average household consists of an elementary family which maintains itself through the combined work of its members on a piece of land they hold. In the dry season, when cultivation is not possible in some parts of the area, the grown-up members seek jobs such as wood collecting and selling, clearing of fields for merchants who want to engage in cultivation, and other types of short-term labor. There is an increasing rate of migration of young men to towns and the Mechanical Crop Production Schemes areas in search of labor, from which they send part of their income home.

Each village has its shaykh, who is selected from the group of early settlers of the place, and whose duty it is to collect taxes, out of which he is paid a small percentage (10 percent). The village shaykh is under the authority of an umda, who is one of the Abu Rūf elite. Each village has one or more shops, and in some cases markets of considerable size have developed.

The Sedentary Elite

From the brief history of landownership in the area, it can be seen that the only landowners who settled on the land with a defined body of followers were the religious leaders. In giving them estates, the Funj sultans not only wanted their blessings, but rightly estimated their significance at the time.[19] The religious men realized how delicate their position was. They tried consistently to emphasize the distinction between themselves and the political leader in the area (whether a sultan or a tribal leader), and between themselves and the common people. The most important thing was to remain neutral in political disputes. This enabled them to play the role of mediators between the different ethnic groups of the sedentary population in the villages as well as between the sedentaries and the nomads. Tribal leaders sought their help and maintained good relationships with them. Most of the transactions between the nomads and the villagers either passed through their hands or were made in the vicinity of their homes, which was considered sacred territory. In this way their neutrality paid off in terms of social and economic power. For a long time they remained the only prosperous elite group among the sedentary people. By converting their social and economic power into political power through attaching themselves to the governing bodies during the Funj and the Turkish rule, they were able to hold their land estates and to become the only decision-making bodies in the villages.

One of the famous families of religious men in the Funj area is the Rawajab family. They claim an Asharf descent[20] and follow the Sammania Order. They taught the Korān and Shari^{c}a law during the Turkish rule and had three Masīds (place for teaching the Korān)--two on the bank of the Blue Nile south of Abu Hugar and one on the plains at al-Mazmum.

The neutrality of religious men on the state level was no longer possible in the early days of the Mahdist revolt. Religious leaders were forced to join the struggle for power between the Mahdists and the Turkish administration, and had to take a side. The Rawajab family leaders joined the Mahdi and led the revolt in the southern part of the Gezira. They were joined by some of the Rufāᶜa al-Hoi nomads, and all moved west to meet the Mahdi in Kordofan after the fall of its capital (El Obeid).

The Mahdiya (1883-1898) was basically opposed to the religious principles advocated by the religious elites. Like many other leading religious families, the Rawajab did not teach or have followers during the Mahdiya because the Funj area was almost depopulated.

The Anglo-Egyptian Condominium had a policy of close supervision of religious leaders in its early days, so that they could not build up a following and lead a revolt. All the political power was in the hands of the tribal leaders (the Abu Rūf family). Although the religious family of the Rawajab reestablished itself, its significance as a power elite was reduced to a minimum, which it maintained only by attaching itself to the tribal leaders through marriage.[21]

By this time another elite group began to emerge. Ethnically this group was constituted of individuals who moved as small merchants from different parts of the northern Sudan. It carefully built up economic power by controlling trade in villages on the banks of the Blue Nile, and gradually extended its economic influence to the villages on the plains. It established chains of small shops by setting up family members in business or entering into partnerships with well-to-do villagers. Some of these chains cover seven or more villages.

These merchants also took advantage of opportunities to invest in various small projects that developed in the area, such as a flour mill, a bakery, etc. But their significance in nazirate politics up to the early 1950's was minor, and they sought alliances with the tribal leaders and played the political game on the basis of the rules laid down by these leaders. With the establishment of the Abu Hugar council (1953), a new arena was opened, and they had a chance to convert the economic power they had accumulated into political power. They had to go through this process of conversion gradually and create a following to back them. The obvious direction in which to look for supporters was toward the villagers. Through their daily interaction, the merchants had created a debt relationship with most of the villagers, whether on the banks of the Blue Nile or on the plains, through the use of the shayl system.[22] They easily manipulated this relationship to further their interests, and thus acquired a large following. They carefully played the ethnic sedentary groups against the Abu Rūf elite by pointing out--indirectly at the beginning--how the Abu Rūf misused their authority to gain personal benefits. In certain situations the merchants succeeded, and in others they failed.

The emergence of national political parties in the area in the early 1950's led to the climax of the rivalry between the two elites. The Rufā^{c}a al-Hoi and the Abu Rūf family supported the Umma party, while the majority of the sedentary people, led by dominant figures among the merchants, supported other parties. With the rapid development and change in most of the spheres of life in the area, the political game became intense within the fields of the council and national politics. The primary goal became the change of the rules for the benefit of one of the competing rivals. In 1964 the sedentary, led by their merchant elites and supported by some dissatisfied nomads--i.e., the sub-elite from the Rufā^{c}a al-Hoi (mainly Bani Husayn, the traditional rivals of Abu Rūf)--urged the new government to abolish the Native Administration system headed by the Abu Rūf elites. The attack was very strong, but because of political changes in the upper levels of the government machinery and the Abu Rūf elites' flexible tactics and strategic manipulation of their relations to the Umma party leaders, the situation remained unchanged.

The Elites and Information and Value Management

The important role of the various categories of elites can be seen by analyzing a few transactions in the fields of economics and politics. In economic transactions across the boundaries of ethnic groups, the necessity of the elites as middlemen is easily illustrated. A nomad who needs some goods from a village shop might have no money and thus might bring one or two sheep to sell so that he can buy what he needs. This kind of transaction can be considered a marketplace transaction where both the nomad and the merchant are equally subject to the terms of trade with no regard to their ethnic differences. In this sense it is not at all problematic. But if we follow the processes involved until the transaction is completed, we can see that there are different variables and values involved, and that their management involves considerable organization.

Suppose such a transaction takes place in any village within the boundaries of the Rufā^{c}a al-Hoi nazirate of Abu Hugar council. In the large villages such as Abu Hugar, Wad al Nayil, al-Dali, al-Mazmum, etc., there are settled members of the Abu Rūf elites. In other, smaller villages there might be some of the Rufā^{c}a al-Hoi who were forced to settle because they lacked herds. A nomad coming into the village is aware of his identity vis-à-vis the villagers. He arrives with a predetermined idea of the value of his sheep according to what they represent in proportion to his herd. He also has an idea of the value of the goods he wants according to his need for them. He is well aware that the merchant's idea of the value of the sheep will be different from his. This does not prevent the transaction, but leads to bargaining, where each hopes to reach a point where he thinks he is making a profit. To have a good bargaining position, a nomad needs information about prices before entering the transaction. The merchant and the butcher--who often are part of the same business enterprise--have the information he needs, but cannot give it to him because it is one of the assets in such a situation. The nomad's alternative is to seek such information from his settled tribal elite. He visits the leading elite house, pays his respects, and sometimes brings a present of his animal products. There is an exchange of information, where the nomad gives an account of the camp's condition, pasture and water situation, etc. Then he talks about the purpose of his visit and asks for the information he needs about prices. Someone from the elite house might return with him to the merchant's shop or the marketplace where he left the animals.

The bargaining over the price of the animals might take place between the merchant and the nomad directly or through a third person representing the merchant--e.g., the butcher. In such a scene, using Goffman's terms, it may be said that a front and a back stage behavior quickly emerge.[23] After bargaining for a while, the merchant's representative goes back to the shop to further discuss the animal's value with the merchant. If it is the merchant himself who is doing the bargaining, he might call the butcher of the village aside and try to get some estimate of the possible profit he can get if the animal is resold or killed. The back stage for the nomad can also take two forms. He can take aside the man who came with him from the elite house and ask about the prices given for similar animals brought by people he has known or about the possibility of better prices in the next village. Or if nobody is around to answer his questions, he can go back to the elite house to discuss the situation. Then both parties return to the front stage where the animals are and review the bargaining. After a while they settle upon a price.

The next step is to move to the merchant's shop, where the nomad selects the goods he needs. Some of these goods might be produced by the sedentary people, but it is rare that one finds a direct transaction between a nomad and a villager in this area.[24] All have to go through the merchant's shop, since there is a debt relationship between the sedentary villager and his village merchant. If a villager needs a sheep, it is unlikely that he has all the money needed to pay for it when the nomad comes to the village. The only way for him to get it is by letting the merchant buy it and then buy it from the merchant on credit after allowing him a reasonable profit.

With a few variations, this is how such transactions normally proceed in the villages. There are cases in the four large villages (Abu Hugar, Wad al Nayil, al-Dali, and al-Mazmum) where a rich nomad has invested his money in consumer goods and has become a settled merchant with part of his family still moving with the rest of the nomads. In such a case the nomads from his old farig can go directly to him instead of to the tribal elite because they know that he understands their ideas of the value of goods transacted, and he will usually be on their side in transactions involving settled people. But this does not happen in all situations. The nomads know that even if a Rufāᶜa al-Hoi merchant is taking their side he must make some profit. It is uncertainty about the amount of profit made in these cases that makes them seek the help of the tribal elite. Also, some doubt arises as to whether such a Rufāᶜa al-Hoi merchant is still adhering to their ideas of the values of animals and market goods, or if his attachment to the business and the village life has changed his attitudes.

With reference to the non-Rufāᶜa al-Hoi merchants, the nomad's idea, which is often openly expressed, is that the merchants are there to exploit them and become rich by cheating them. The merchants demand high prices for the goods they control because they know that the nomads cannot do without such goods, while they offer low prices for the animals, which they know the nomads have to sell to get these consumer goods.

There are cases where there may be no tribal elite in the village and no merchant who was originally a nomad. In such cases the nomad will seek any of the Rufāᶜa al-Hoi who were forced to settle because of economic circumstances, and get information from them. But if this is not possible either, a type of friendly relationship is established between the village merchant (or merchants) and the nomads. Such a relation when found can go far beyond the simple transaction described above. The merchant might buy a number of animals from the nomads and leave them with their herds. The nomads, when moving near the village, can leave with the merchant any of his animals which are weak and cannot cope with the movement of the rest of the herd. The merchant can also give a few goods to one of his nomad friends and enable him to establish a small moving shop in his camp cluster. (There are less than five of these shops among all the Rufāᶜa al-Hoi camps.)

In making his annual animal sale (gelba), a nomad goes to large towns outside the Abu Hugar council area--places like al-Roseires, Singa, Sennar, Kosti, or Madeni. There marketplace situations governed by the law of supply and demand can be seen to operate. Yet still there is a man on whom the nomads depend for price information. This man is known by the term dhamin. He is the one who guarantees the transactions and is responsible for locating the nomads if any complications develop later. He is paid a certain percentage. He is normally from the Rufā^c^a al-Hoi tribe and/or is connected to the elite in one way or another. (The system of dhamin holds for other tribes in the Sudan.)[25]

In transactions of a political nature, the role of the elite is so important that the government has found it useful to institutionalize it. This institutionalization takes the form of the top nazirate and umdas' offices, as well as the courts, being dominated by the elites. A considerable number of the sedentary elite beside the Abu Rūf elite take part in settling disputes between the different ethnic groups in the area. In cases of crop damage by the nomads' herds, villagers and nomads' committees consisting of the nomads' sub-elite and some of the villagers or their elites are set up by the council or the nazir to settle the disputes. The most important role the elites play is the representation of the masses to other ethnic groups and to the government authority in a way the administrators recognize. This, as Barth states, "touches on a very fundamental problem in the organization of 'plural' societies"--that is, the problem of contact between different ethnic groups where workable mechanisms that can make them comparable are needed to bridge the gaps.[26]

The problem of solving conflicts in the Rufā^c^a al-Hoi nazirate--as in Fars--can only be approached by "channelling these conflicts through administrative superstructures which bridge this difference by transforming the interest and the social units concerned to a point where they become comparable and thus able to communicate."[27] It is not only in the cases noted above but also in the council chambers that the elites serve as representatives of the masses.

The processes involved in political transactions are much more complicated than the economic ones discussed above. The interests and complaints of the nomad masses are expressed in their own idioms to their tribal elites through an intermediary group--the sub-elite. These views, if they are to be taken into the council arena, must be put into much more sophisticated language. This is because in this arena the tribal elite are dealing with government officials, some of whom are highly educated and have little knowledge of the nomads' idioms and problems. The problem of understanding idioms and modes of life also arises in contacts with the sedentary elite, where the major issue is the increasing competition over land. There is an increasing demand from the sedentary elite for the use of the grazing lands of the nomads to establish mechanical crop production schemes. There is also a conflict between the tribal and sedentary elites on this point because these schemes threaten the existence of the gum gardens which are a basic economic resource necessary for the continuity of the tribal elite as a dominant group. The question of leaving certain places on the banks of the Blue Nile as water spots for the nomads' herds also leads to much debate. Other issues--such as equal distribution of development projects over the area in such a way as to give equal benefits for both nomads and sedentary populations--make up a major part of the controversy in this area.

When issues are discussed and decisions reached, the process is reversed all the way down to the masses. The merchant elite play a similar role to that of the tribal elite, except that they come as representatives of a much more heterogeneous population whose interests differ markedly. In many ways, the merchant elite is concerned--far more than the tribal elite--with their interests as individuals. This is mainly because, unlike the nomads, they operate in a situation where a number of ethnic groups interact, and they do not need to commit themselves to one or another group. A very important point here is the difference in the definition of "power" between the sedentary and the tribal elites. In the sedentary situation, power is gained through the accumulation of wealth and control of economic resources, and fits the Weberian definition of the concept: "It is simply the actor's opportunity to impose his will on another, even against the other's resistance."[28] It is only because of the shayl system that the sedentary population accept the representation of the sedentary elite and give them support in both the council and national political arenas. But they make it clear, on all possible occasions, that it is against their will, and that they have no alternative because they depend for their living upon these elites.

The concept of power in the tribal situation has the same definition, but more than that, it is ideologically legitimized through the patrilineal descent ideology. A further difference is that the nomad masses accept the dominance of their elites because they realize their inability to act in political arenas outside the tribal structure. Though there might be some resentment concerning the way the tribal elites treat certain issues, and the nomads may consider other alternatives, they do not question the legitimacy of the elite. In 1964 the question of the legitimacy of the actions of their elites was raised. A few expressed certain doubts, but later they realized they were misled by the sedentary elite to take a political stand which was against their own interests.

Through their authority over the masses, whether sedentary or nomad, the elites keep these masses far from the arenas where political decisions are made--i.e., the council. Also, needing the masses as sources of support, each group of elites tries to keep its masses out of touch with the others. It is through the creation of boundaries between the masses that the elites maintain themselves as powerful groups.

In the national arena the nomads have managed to maintain unity. With the exception of the leading family of the Abu Rūf, which has always provided the candidates for its constituency, the Rufā^{c}a al-Hoi tribe are strictly Ansar (followers of the Mahdi). They have solidly backed the Umma party on national political issues. The elite group, aware of the fact that its rivals in the tribe (the Bani Husayn) could use its non-Ansar status to undermine its political leadership, has always pretended to be Ansar.

The sedentary elite and their masses do not have such unity, and thus they have backed different candidates. The merchants in the area are the regional representatives of the Umma party, and they have used the net of their relations with the people to get their support. Only in a few cases have they managed to put up candidates, who were then easily defeated by the Abu Rūf candidate.

Conclusions

The lack of understanding of nomad-sedentary relations arises mainly from what men of education and planners assume about the nomadic style of life. They are exponents of sedentary civilization who regard the word "nomad" as a term of abuse.[29] They think that the best way to improve the standard of living of nomads is by settling them. In advocating this, they face the question of integrating different ethnic groups on both the cultural and social levels. They eventually realize that they don't know enough about the relationships between these groups. A partial answer lies in understanding the roles of the elites in these communities.

In their position as mediators and value managers between their two communities, the tribal and sedentary elites have access to information which the masses on both sides lack. One serious mistake planners make is thinking that all information is carried down to the masses. The elites have their own economic and political interests which would be affected if all information were passed on. Therefore they manage it in such a way that their interests are secured. Each category of the elite knows that the others are doing this, and that to keep their positions they have to support each other.

Debates in council chambers over different facilities become debates between nomads and sedentary people, and sometimes are carried so far that they appear to show that these groups can no longer coexist under the same administrative body. But in the end, compromises are reached, and most of the issues are settled. Reviewing these issues, it can be seen that compromises have been based on a reasonable sharing of the rewards from transactions. The greater part of these rewards go to the elites of both sides.

These elites are the entrepreneurs[30] of the area, and their competition is over opportunities that come up through the central government's plans for development, as well as other sources. These opportunities are far beyond the reach of the masses because they don't have the capital, the skill, or the ability to establish contacts and good relations with government officials. Most of the time the tribal and sedentary elites cooperate in these matters. This was especially true in the past, when the sedentary elite's power was not significant enough to be threatening. But through the change brought about by national politics after independence (1956), the competition started to become much more serious. The economic power of the sedentary elite in the area increased rapidly through their participation in the mechanized crop production schemes that took over most of the Rufā^{c}a al-Hoi communal lands, as well as the control of gum prices, which is the only source of cash income among the nomads. The fact that entrepreneurs from other parts of the Sudan, including some of the ministers of the former military regime of 1958-1964, entered as scheme owners gave the sedentary elite new economically and politically powerful allies. This made them think of changing the rules of the game in rural council politics in such a way that they could have authority for making decisions concerning all the important issues in the area--especially land.

In both the sedentary and nomadic ethnic groups, a kind of authoritarian elite has grown up with which planners have cooperated and from whom they have sought advice to implement their new programs. But these elites have partly defeated the purposes of planned programs on the economic level, for example, by excluding or discouraging enterprising individuals from the masses.

It is only through the analysis of simple daily transactions, whether in the field of domestic economy or politics, that an understanding of the nomad-sedentary relation can be achieved. The simplest transactions show the presence of a number of processes to which we normally do not pay much attention. It is through the pattern exhibited by these processes that a model for nomad-sedentary interaction can be generated. Through all this it can be seen that the elite play a very important role, however hard they try to serve their own interests. Through an analysis of their role as middlemen, we come to the conclusion that they manipulate communications and change the value of information. In this way they keep the different ethnic groups apart by defining the situation for them, as well as by keeping the government from the scene. By doing this, they make their presence as a bridge a necessity.

Footnotes

[1]Fredrik Barth: Principles of Social Organization in Southern Kurdistan (Oslo: Brödrene Jörgensen, 1953); "Ecological Relationships of Ethnic Groups in Swat, North Pakistan," American Anthropologist, Vol. 58, 1956; Nomads of South Persia (Oslo: Universitetsforlaget, 1964); and "Competition and Symbiosis in Northeast Baluchistan," Folk, Vol. 6, 1964; G. Håland, "Economic Determinants in Ethnic Processes" in F. Barth, ed., Ethnic Groups and Boundaries: The Social Organization of Culture Difference (Boston: Little, Brown, and Co., 1969); and P. Salzman, ed., Comparative Studies of Nomadism and Pastoralism (Special Issue of Anthropological Quarterly), 1971.

[2]Fredrik Barth, "Models of Social Organization," Royal Anthropological Institute Occasional Papers, 1966.

[3]C. Wright Mills, The Power Elite (New York: Oxford University Press, 1956), p. 23.

[4]A. Cohen, "Political Anthropology: The Analysis of the Symbolism of Power Relations," Man, 1969.

[5]S.F. Nadel, "The Concept of Social Elites," International Social Science Bulletin, Vol. VIII, No. 3 (1956).

[6]The concept of the elite has been applied to the political structure of a nomadic tribe by Talal Asad in his treatment of the Kababish (The Kababish Arabs [London: Hurst, 1970]). Barth talks about the sedentary elites in Fars and observes that the nomads' chief is treated as their equal (Barth, Nomads . . .).

[7]Nadel.

[8]Y.F. Hasan, The Arabs and the Sudan (Aldine: Edinburgh University Press, 1967), p. 159.

[9]First Population Census of Sudan, 1955-6 (Khartoum, 1958).

[10]For more information on the Rufāᶜa al-Hoi economy and politics, see Abdel Ghaffar M. Ahmed, "The Role of the Sedentary Population in the Rufāᶜa al-Hoi Politics," Sudan Notes and Records, Vol. 52, 1971, and "The Rufāᶜa al-Hoi Economy" in Cunnison and James, eds., Essays in Sudan Ethnography (London: Hurst, 1972).

[11]The khalwa is the meeting place for the camp cluster's male members and where male guests are entertained. It is located a short distance from the tents in the direction of the main track leading to the cluster. It can be a tent, or a shelter made of straw, or a big tree.

[12]Abdel Ghaffar M. Ahmed, "The Rufāᶜa al-Hoi Economy . . . ."

[13]James Bruce, Travels to Discover the Source of the Nile (Edinburgh University Press, 1790), p. 497.

[14]R. Hill, On the Frontiers of Islam (New York: Oxford University Press, 1967), pp. 7 and 34.

[15]Rudolf C. Slatin, Fire and Sword in the Sudan (London, 1896), pp. 22-23.

[16]The nazir is the head of the tribe. This term has been administratively recognized since the Turkish rule in the Sudan, together with the term umda. Umda means a head of an administrative unit composed of a collection of villages, which is known as umudiya. Under the Native Administration system, most of the rural population of the Sudan, settled or nomadic, are divided into nazirates headed by a nazir, and including a number of umudiyas.

[17]Abdel Ghaffar M. Ahmed, "The Role of the Sedentary . . . ."

[18]M.H. Awad, "The Evolution of Landownership in the Sudan," The Middle East Journal, Vol. XXV, No. 2 (1971).

[19]Abu Selim M.I., ed., Some Land Certificates from the Funj (Khartoum: Sudan Research Unit, 1967), p. 35.

[20]They trace their descent back to the family of the prophet Muhammad.

[21]The present head of the extended family of the Rawajab is married to the daughter of the ex-nazir of the Rufāᶜa al-Hoi. The marriage was contracted while that nazir was still in power.

[22]The shayl system is one by which "credit is extended by the merchant-lender in the form of advances in money or kind against the next crop. Several types of shayl are practiced--the oldest form is an advance of grain or seed valued at a price substantially above the estimated price at the next harvest. The borrower must settle the loan by returning at harvest time enough grain to make up the money equivalent of the loan" (M.W. Wilmington, "Aspect of Moneylending in Northern Sudan," Middle East Journal, Vol. IX, 1965, p. 141).

[23]Erving Goffman, The Presentation of Self in Everday Life (New York: Anchor Books, 1959).

[24]Direct transactions take place between the group of Rufāᶜa al-Hoi who spend the dry season south of khor Yabus. They take the form of barter: animal products for grain. Their scale is

very small, and they are conducted because the Rufā^c^a al-Hoi are far away from villages that have shops.

[25] See Asad, The Kababish Arabs.

[26] Barth, Nomads of South Persia, p. 77.

[27] Ibid., p. 79.

[28] Quoted from Raymond Aron, Main Currents in Sociological Thought, Vol. II (London: Pelican Books, 1970), p. 236.

[29] I.M. Lewis, "Nomadism: An Anthropological View" (presented to the FAO Conference, Cairo, December 1971).

[30] Although the Abu Rūf elite cannot be such, in the strict meaning of the word, there are a considerable number of them involved in entrepreneur activities themselves or in partnerships with merchants in the area.

THE NOMADIC AND THE SEDENTARY: POLAR COMPLEMENTARIES--NOT POLAR OPPOSITES

Abbas Mohammed

Introduction

Hitherto, the relation between pastoral nomads and their sedentary neighbors or the state at large has been represented by many social anthropologists as one of "polar opposition" rather than "polar complementarity." In a recent paper given at an FAO conference in Cairo, I.M. Lewis makes two points which to me summarize the general attitude of anthropologists to nomad/sedentary-state relations. He says: "Nomads . . . regularly make a defiant parade of all those attributes which they know are most calculated to annoy their sedentary neighbors."[1] He also argues that "the nomad's capricious movements severely curtail his commitment to the state which is, by definition, sedentary and of fixed geographic location."[2]

This essay, in a very limited way, sets out to challenge this prevailing view by examining the socio-economic interaction and interdependence between the pastoral and nonpastoral groups inhabiting the North White Nile region of the Sudan, including the employment of pastoral nomads in cotton-picking in the White Nile schemes.

The nomadic participation as a labor force in cotton-picking amounts to 42 percent of the total hired labor. This figure is computed from a questionnaire distributed in a scheme known as the Rahawat or Sufi scheme. It is one among a group of cotton schemes in the Sufi basin, a low flat land of fertile soil. Most of the cotton schemes in the White Nile area today are government-owned and form a merger known as the White Nile Scheme Board (WNSB). This board has come into being since the building of the Jebel Awlia Dam in 1937; the cotton schemes were developed to provide subsistence and cash for the displaced, dispossessed Arabs whose land was submerged by the river. The schemes numbered about half a dozen by the early 1940's, but today they total more

---

I am indebted to Professor I.M. Lewis for background discussion and encouragement in writing this paper. I would also like to acknowledge the help and critical comments of my colleagues Pamela Constantinides and Jill Shepherd.

than fifteen. Most of the later schemes were built by the mid-1950's, and since then the problem of obtaining the labor force needed in cotton planting, and especially in cotton-picking, has been acute.

The White Nile Arabs have solved the problem by absorbing the "intrinsic surplus labor" in nomadic pastoralism, which has recently been described as "nomads on the waiting list."[3] The absorption of these nomads has provided them with a source of cash which could be used to purchase animals, helping them to be instituted in nomadic pastoralism, and thus contribute to the continuity of the pastoral economy. But they also contribute to the sedentary economy by becoming a major element in production. As a result, the pastoral and sedentary economies have become coordinated to a point where the continuity of each is dependent to a considerable extent upon the other. When we consider that cotton enterprise is not only basic to the economy of the "neighboring sedentary people" but also of the state at large (cotton is the main, if not the only, national cash crop), the significance of the nomads' contribution to state development can be clearly appreciated. The nomadic contribution is threefold: they contribute to their own economy, to that of their sedentary neighbors, and to that of the state at large.

Other social interaction has resulted from this economic coordination. On the farm site where the two families of the sedentary employer and the nomadic employee settle together during the cotton-picking period, social interaction in terms of friendship and reciprocity takes place. The interaction on the farm site is extended into even a wider network of reciprocal obligations. Thus in ritual periods the two families--the sedentary and the nomadic--exchange visits, payments, and gifts.

Let us start by considering briefly the contextual framework in which these processes are taking place.

Contextual Framework: Pastoral and Sedentary Groups

Dar Hassania Nazarate (dissolved in 1969-70 by the Sudan government), which is coterminous with the North White Nile Rural Council, covers an area of approximately 76,000 square miles (100 miles north to south and 70 miles east to west) and has a population of about 500,000. It is inhabited by a multitude of Muslim Arab tribes with varying modes of livelihood: sedentary, semi-nomadic, and nomadic. Along the riverbelt of the White Nile, the dominant physical feature of the region, live the Hassania and Hissinat (of Kawahla origin) and a few others. These tribes obtain their living from sedentary cultivation--mainly cotton and *dura* (grain). Before the building of Jebel Awlia Dam in 1937, these groups were semi-nomadic, practicing both animal husbandry and cultivation of a highly sedentary nature. Since the construction of the dam and the rise of cotton schemes, they have become completely sedentarized.

On the fringes of the Dar or in the hinterland to the west of the Nile live a number of small tribes, such as the Magdia, the Kawahla, the Shiwaihat, the Kurtan, and the Shenabla.[4] These are pastoral nomads who depend for their living mainly on animal husbandry. They keep camels, cattle, sheep, and goats. Milk is their staple diet, but they supplement this with dura--both by cultivating it on a limited scale locally and by purchasing it from their sedentary neighbors.

Prior to the Turko-Egyptian regime in the Sudan (1820-1885), there were hostilities and raids between some of these nomadic groups and the once semi-sedentary Hassania. But this hostility should be understood in its historical context rather than be attributed to nomadism as such, or be seen--as Lewis would see it--as an "intrinsic feature of pastoral nomadism."[5] The hostility was due mainly to the fact that some of these groups were pushed to the fringes of the region or driven out completely by the Hassania when they first moved into this area from the northern Sudan in about the seventeenth century.

However, the stability provided by the formation of a national state from the Turko-Egyptian era to the Mahdist period (1885-1898), followed by the Anglo-Egyptian Condominium (1899), and then an independent national government (1956), has made hostility largely a thing of the past. But other factors have contributed to peaceful coexistence between the two sectors.

First, with the rise of the Mahdist revolution, both sectors--nomads and the semi-sedentary--joined the Mahdist cause and became closely allied through it.[6] When the Mahdist cause was revived in the 1920's and 1930's by Sayyid Abdel Rahman al-Mahdi, both sectors joined the "Ansar Brotherhood," which later developed into the national Ummah political party.

Second, the nomads and their sedentary neighbors were brought together under one native administration system from the late 1920's until the system was abolished in 1969-70. Together they formed the Dar Hassania Nazarate, headed by the Hassania _Nazir_ (paramount chief).

Third, market relations have developed between the two groups since the turn of the century. Important markets like Shigeig and Helba have become focal points for commercial interaction between the nomads and the riverain folk.

Since 1937, when Jebel Awlia Dam was built, the cotton schemes have emerged and the Hassania have become a highly sedentary people. For a while it seemed likely that this would result in a wide gap between the pastoral and the now sedentary people because there would no longer be the interaction and close proximity of semi-nomadism. However, the cultivation of cotton and the rise of the need for labor, especially for cotton-picking, has bridged this gap, and the two sectors have become coordinated by an ongoing economic interdependence.

In the discussion which follows, we will be considering this developed coordination between pastoral groups and the sedentary population. Since the data presented here are derived from only one area, known as the Sufi basin, we will be considering the coordination between only certain of the pastoral groups--namely, the Kawahla, Magdia, and Shiwaihat--and those riverain sedentary people who get their living from the scheme in this area known as the Rahawat or Sufi scheme. It is through close territorial and social proximity that the nomadic groups we are concerned with here have become involved in cotton-picking and affected by its socioeconomic repercussions, but the interaction represented reflects a pattern common throughout the White Nile area, and is not by any means a special or exceptional case.

Sedentary Economy and the Need for Imported Labor

The economy of the riverain Arabs depends mainly on the cultivation of cotton as a cash crop and dura for subsistence. The cultivation of these crops takes place in schemes, which are mainly government-owned. An individual scheme consists of a number of hawashas, or farm plots, allocated to individual tenants. The scheme we are referring to here--the Rahawat or Sufi scheme--has about 400 hawashas altogether. A hawasha consists of 18 feddans divided into three plots of six feddans each, so that a rotational system of cotton/dura/fallow can be followed. The Rahawat scheme is run on a tenancy basis: the government provides the land, irrigation, technical supervision, agricultural equipment, and necessities and arranges for marketing, and the individual farmer provides the manual labor needed for the various activities on his farm. From the sale of the cotton produce, the farmer gets a certain percentage--about 40 percent of the net profit from the sale of the crop. He is also given the whole dura crop for his own subsistence, and the government does not charge him anything for it. However, most of the agricultural activities in both cotton and dura cultivation need more labor and more attention than can be provided by an individual farmer alone or with the aid of his nuclear family. The need for extra labor is met by wage labor, and the scheme provides loans for farmers to finance or assist in financing this hired labor--but for cotton only, not for dura. In most of these agricultural activities, the need for casual labor has

Table 1

SOURCES OF LABOR FOR DURA AND COTTON AGRICULTURAL ACTIVITIES FOR 41 CASES IN SUFI VILLAGE: 1969-1970[a]

	Free Labor		Wage Labor		
				Non-Village	
	Nuclear Family	Relatives and Friends	Village	Other Villages	Nomads
Dura Activities					
Sowing	29	--	10	2	--
Clearance	7	2	24	6	2
Kadib (thinning out)	32	--	9	--	--
Cotton Activities					
Sowing	23	--	15	2	1
Clearance	1	1	18	17	4
Shalikh (thinning out)	32	--	8	1	--
Picking	--	--	5	19	17

[a]A limitation of this table is that it refers to incidences only and not to the size of the labor force involved--i.e., the number of persons.

become so great that an imported labor force from either other sedentary villages or pastoral nomads has become indispensable.

Table 1 shows the significance of hired labor, especially imported labor, in both cotton and dura cultivation. The table includes data from 41 farms, and shows how labor needs are met from the various sources of nuclear family, relations and friends, the village, and imported labor, which is divided into two categories: other sedentary villages and neighboring pastoral nomads. The table shows (a) that nomads are imported mainly for cotton-picking and (b) that a small number of nomads are engaged in other agricultural activities--primarily cotton and dura clearance. (It should be observed that a limitation of this table is that it refers to the distribution of incidences and not to the size of the labor force involved--i.e., the number of persons.)

Because the special participation of pastoral nomads is so great during cotton-picking, Table 2 has been computed to show the percentage of the labor force provided by pastoral nomads

Table 2

NUMBER OF PERSONS AND PERCENTAGE OF THE HIRED LABOR FORCE PROVIDED BY PASTORAL NOMADS FOR COTTON-PICKING IN SUFI VILLAGE IN 1970[a]

	Source of Labor			
	Village	Other Villages	Pastoral Nomads	Total
Number of persons	22	73	69	164
Percentage of labor force	13.5	44.5	42.0	100

[a]Data are for 43 cases--i.e., 43 hawashas or plots.

in relation to other sources of labor for cotton-picking in Sufi village in 1970.

Table 3 shows the contribution--in actual numbers and as a percentage of the total nomadic participation--of each of the main nomadic groups which participate in cotton-picking in Sufi village.

As noted earlier, the scheme provides loans for farmers to help them in financing wage labor. Thus in 1970, for example, loans given to farmers averaged £S1.2 for sowing, £S6 for clearance, £S1.6 for the late clearance (shalikh), and £S8.5 for picking. The scheme also gives the farmer two installments of £S4 each during cotton cultivation to help him manage until the crop is sold. Each farmer has an account with the scheme; at the end of the cultivation year when the crop is sold, his expenses are subtracted from the total income from his crop, and he gets 40 percent of the net profit.

In 1969-70 the Rahawat scheme provided about £S3,400 for farmers to meet the costs of wage labor for cotton-picking alone. A very rough estimate of the cash advantages which come to pastoral nomads, who constitute about 42 percent of the total labor force, would be £S1428.[7]

Cotton-Picking and Type of Labor Needed

In cotton and dura cultivation the annual labor schedule is something like this: sowing--about August; clearance and late clearance--September and October; dura harvest--November and December; cotton-picking--January to March.

Table 3

CONTRIBUTION OF VARIOUS NOMADIC GROUPS IN COTTON-PICKING SHOWN AS PERCENTAGES OF THE TOTAL NOMADIC PARTICIPATION

	Nomadic Group				Total Nomadic Labor Force
	Magdia	Kawahla	Shiwaihat	Other	
Number of persons	24	20	16	9	69
Percentage of labor force	35.0	29.0	23.0	13.0	100.0

Cotton-picking is simple: it requires no special skill or training. However, it does require a certain care and patience, for if the cotton boll is not taken off in the right way, part of it is wasted by being left behind; and if the boll is not pulled carefully it may be dropped on the ground, getting dirty and resulting in a low quality of cotton. (These are the basic rules of cotton-picking, and a nomad or other laborer is so instructed.) Each farmer has a small weighing machine to weigh and record the amount collected by each laborer, who is then paid at the end of each day, week, or picking session--usually a fortnight. After this period the farm is watered for some time, and another fortnight must elapse before it is ready for re-picking. Altogether an average farm needs about three sessions spreading over about two months to complete picking.

There are two categories of cotton pickers (or _logat_), known locally as _nuzal_ (residents or settlers) and _barshata_ ("pick-and-run laborers"). [Literally the word _barshata_ denotes secret or nonlegal possession or ownership of property or money.] Nuzal are contracted pickers, and barshata are noncontracted. A barshati agrees to come and collect cotton for you today but may not come tomorrow. He is one who "plays the market," seeing where there is plenty of cotton to be picked for a high wage. Usually this category of casual laborers is made up of co-villagers who know the people, their farms, and the wage market more thoroughly than an outsider could.

Nuzal, on the other hand, are pickers who make a tacit agreement with the farmer on the following premises:

1. During such time of cotton-picking as is prescribed by the farmer (usually between January and March), the client-to-be and his family, if any, will render themselves available in the service of the farmer whereby they settle on his farm and work for him in cotton-picking.

2. During the prescribed period the client will not work for anybody else except during the watering sessions when the client becomes temporarily redundant.

3. The farmer will provide the client with:
   (a) Transport or the money for it
   (b) A straw hut for him to live in on the farm
   (c) One kaila (a measure of dura) and ten piastres per head for each member of the family acting as a picker
   (d) A certain rate for picking--about 15 piastres per quantar (equivalent to 100 pounds of weight).

The nuzal category of pickers is made up mainly of outsiders who are either from neighboring sedentary villages or are neighboring pastoral nomads. Because the nuzal contract has guarantees for the outsider, it is especially appealing to the nomad, who gets free grain for his subsistence in addition to cash. He may otherwise have to sell some of his own animals, if he has any, to get grain for subsistence.

We should note that the contract is based primarily on trust and mutual need, and is sanctioned mainly by the employer not paying the client anything if he fails to appear during cotton-picking time. There is also the sanction of the possible inclusion of the client on a blacklist, so that he will not be approached by others. Such things seldom if ever occur, however, because a man fails to show up only if he has an acceptable reason like the death of a relative or sickness. While working on the farm--that is, during picking--he cannot breach the contract because his employer might make him permanently redundant, since other people would decline to employ him. (See the section on recruitment for other sanctions behind the contract.)

These factors involved in the contractual transaction are especially significant for the pastoralist-sedentary relationship, for they both presuppose and promote mutual trust and goodwill between the two interacting partners.

In the following section we will show how pastoral nomads manage to supply this considerable labor force for their sedentary neighbors, what categories of nomads are supplying it, and what the economic and social repercussions of the relationship are.

Nomadic Pastoralism and the Seasonal Surplus of Labor

Most nomads or pastoralists have certain phases of idleness during their annual economic cycle. It is a period of relaxation characteristic, for instance, of the Kababish Dumur[8] (summer season) and the like. But there are certain sectors or categories of nomads who are more idle, or idle for longer, than the others. Indeed, among some pastoralists a few people are left behind all the year round. These include not only the elderly and the sick, but also usually the very poor people who have no animals (or very few). Among the pastoral Kawahla in the White Nile these are called admanin (wealthless). However, there is nearly always a peak in the pastoral cycle when labor is needed from virtually everyone. This is characteristic of the Kharif (rainy season) in the Sudan. Then even the poorest are urged by their kinsfolk to join the seasonal migration which utilizes the kharif pastures and water, and there is a general tendency for full employment at this time. But with the advent of winter, there is less need for watering of animals, and therefore less labor is required. A category of unemployed begins to emerge and increases gradually till it reaches its peak in the summer when everyone returns home.

In a recent FAO conference held in Cairo, Nader Afshar Naderi of Iran has described these temporarily unemployed pastoralists as "nomads on the waiting list." In the Iranian context, nomads on the waiting list are characteristic of summer only. In the White Nile case, however, they are in evidence during the period from midwinter till the end of summer, because the decreased need for watering in winter gradually forces some labor out of pastoralism. These people are neither completely nomadic nor completely sedentary, but spend a part of the year waiting to be practicing nomads.

What has been outlined so far is an intrinsic part of the nomadic pastoralism prevailing among the White Nile pastoral Arabs, such as the groups we are interested in here: the Kawahla, the Magdia, and the Shiwaihat. Now let us briefly sketch the main migratory features of these pastoralists.

These tribes have permanent dwellings which they refer to as dumur, or summer dwellings. They are built around ids (wells or watering centers), some of which are constructed in a modern fashion or built by the government. The Magdia and the Kawahla have dumur centers around Shigeig Id, and the Shiwaihat near Jebel Tuis.

In the kharif they move westward to the boundaries of Dar Kababish to exploit the pastures and water of the early showers and the main kharif. They also occasionally practice goz cultivation during this time. (They grow dura, sesame, and ful.) In the winter (or shita) they come back toward home, but before reaching it they stop to utilize the physical resources they left untouched while they hurriedly moved westward earlier. During this time, especially in midwinter, less work is needed, since animals do not need frequent watering from the shallow wells or ids in the khairan (watercourses or streams). This is especially true of camels, which can be left unwatered for a fortnight or more. As a result, some kinsmen formerly taken along for their labor or the poor with few animals are either unemployed or form a category of disguised unemployment. Some indeed may end their journey and go home before the summer, when all the rest will follow. It is this category of people--who wait for the next kharif for their labor to be needed or to acquire some or some more animals qualifying themselves for pastoralism--whom we have described as "nomads on the waiting list." It is this category of redundant people who have found in cotton-picking along the river a new market for their labor and an opportunity to shorten the waiting time before becoming full-time pastoralists through their ability to change earned cash into animals and meet their need for cash (for taxation or market goods) without selling from the limited stock, if any, which they possess.

Recruitment and the Factors of Physical and Social Proximity

To account for the separate needs of each system, the nomadic and the sedentary, is not enough to account for how each becomes aware of the circumstances of the internal system of and its need for the other. For example, each group has to make its approach to the other at the right time and place.

Thus the approach of nomads by the now sedentary people who wish to recruit them for labor in cotton-picking involves an awareness by the riverain people of the built-in redundancy of the pastoral economy. The riverain people approach the pastoral groups for fresh recruits toward the end of November--that is, at the beginning of winter--so as to get early information about who will be redundant and who will be back in the dumur when the demand for his labor has ended. The role of those already serving on the cotton list as pickers is very important because they act as brokers between the sedentary farmers and future pickers. They know their people and their circumstances much better than the sedentary farmers could, and--of most significance--they give fresh contracts solid backing, for both old and new recruits are members of a small kin group and a breach of contract will be negatively sanctioned by that relationship.

In the following we can give only a very brief outline of the main factors which have promoted the awareness of mutual need and the possibilities arising from it:

1. Territorial and geographical proximity: Both sectors lie within easy reach of each other, the Magdia and Kawahla having their permanent settlements within 20 miles of the riverain schemes. The development of transport following

the rise of the White Nile schemes has made the journey between the two even shorter--about half an hour or so in a bus.

2. Preexisting market relations: Since the turn of the century Shigeig market, which is very near to Shigeig Id (the watering center), has developed as a main focal point of interaction between these nomadic groups and the semi-sedentary and sedentary inhabitants of the White Nile. Animals, cash, grain, and market goods are regularly exchanged between the two sectors.

3. Socio-cultural homogeneity: The sedentary riverain people of today were themselves semi-sedentary or semi-nomadic till the late 1930's when Jebel Awlia Dam was built, followed by the cotton schemes. Similarly, some of the pastoral groups involved (for example, the Shiwaihat and Magdia) were riverain folk in about the seventeenth century, but they were forced to move away from the river when the Hassania came into the region. The Kawahla are thought of as closely related to the Hassania, who often speak of themselves as Kawahla.

   Thus there are close socio-cultural ties between the sedentary and nomadic groups, and ethnic boundaries are minimal. This is not to say that there are not institutional differences or that there is no tribal feeling. But in contrast to some parts of the Sudan where nomads are seen as a different species of people (and referred to as bedu or Arabs--that is, uncouth and barbarian), in the White Nile the distinction between pastoral nomads and sedentary cultivators is shown in the idiom of referring to the two sectors as arab al-bahgyim (Arabs of the animals) and arab al-bahar (Arabs of the river) respectively--references to modes of livelihood and their contextual frameworks.

4. Administrative and religious unity: Both sectors are part of the former Dar Hassania Nazarate or, as it exists today, the North White Nile Rural Council. In the past the two sectors were connected by one wakilship or deputy nazirship with its headquarters near Sufi village at a place called Wad Nimr. (The overall nazarate headquarters were at Dueim.) Interaction between the two sectors has been accelerated by the institutionalization of the native administration since the late 1920's.

   Both sectors were devout followers of the Mahdist cause and its revival in the White Nile in the 1920's and 1930's and both sectors consequently became supporters of the Ummah (or Mahdist) political party.

Socio-Economic Repercussions

The high rate of nomadic participation in cotton-picking to meet the need for labor is indispensable to a sedentary economy dependent on cotton cultivation. In the White Nile the use of pastoral nomads in cotton-picking has given rise to some economic and social repercussions of great significance to nomad-sedentary relations. To elaborate:

Nomadic pastoral economy and sedentary cultivation are coordinated and integrated to a great extent, so that the continuity of each depends on the other to a high degree. The fact that 42 percent of the hired labor for cotton-picking is provided by pastoral nomads means that nomads are no longer mere consumers of sedentary goods (e.g., grain) but are also a main element in sedentary economic production. Cotton-picking is the backbone of cotton cultivation, and both the quality and quantity of cotton obtained depend on it.

We have seen from Table 1 that there is a persistent need for labor throughout the agricultural year in Sufi village for both dura and cotton. For cotton-picking the need is especially critical, because when the time for it is due the local labor is already exhausted by having had to cope with the other agricultural activities relating to dura and cotton cultivation (see Table 1).

For the pastoral nomads there are significant effects. The new source of cash enables them, in good productive years, to buy animals and gradually qualify themselves to be fully incorporated into the pastoral economy or, in our terms, to be moved from the "waiting list" into the "active list" of pastoralism. They get dura as a bonus for their labor, and are therefore not forced to sell their animals to get dura in exchange. The new source of cash also enables them to meet their own needs for cash, such as for taxation or for general market goods.

No doubt the process by which a nomad on the waiting list uses this source of cash to be incorporated into full nomadism through the accumulation of livestock is a long and gradual one. It is very difficult to determine what one can call the "waiting expectancy" of a redundant pastoralist--especially when one has done his research among the sedentary rather than the nomadic sector and is inevitably speaking from a sedentary point of view. But I am familiar with at least two cases where nomadic cotton-pickers have ceased to come for cotton-picking because they have accumulated enough wealth to enable them to be fully employed as pastoralists for the whole year. One of these cases is very significant, and I will briefly sketch it here because it is connected with some points I would like to make.

THE NOMADIC AND THE SEDENTARY: POLAR COMPLEMENTARIES

A certain man of the Amria lineage called Mohammed Ali came to me in the summer of 1970 to ask me to take him, his family, and near kin in my Landrover to some people in the Shigeig area. When I asked him who these people were and why he wished to go there, he told me that they were the Kawahla people who came and picked cotton for him. He said that a relative of the Kawahla had died and that they wanted to make a reciprocal visit because these people had come to see them the previous year when a relative of theirs had died. I eventually went with them, and became aware of the closeness of the relationship between the two families, who seemed to know each other very well.

In December 1970 when the time came for approaching nomads for contractual labor, I asked Mohammed Ali whether he was going to have the same people again. He replied, "No, I'm having someone else through their recommendation. I have realized since last year or even the year before that they might not be coming much longer. You know, these people are getting rich now. I don't think they will think of cotton-picking again. Anyhow, God only knows!" I then asked him how long these people had worked for him, and he replied that it might be five or six years or more.

This case illustrates two important points: first, how through cotton-picking there is a tendency for the institution of redundant nomads into full-time pastoralism; second, how a contractual relationship between sedentary employer and nomadic employee can give rise to a wider social network of relationships involving the two respective families and carried on through channels of reciprocal obligations, by exchanging visits and payments at times of ritual periods. It is interesting to see how this process has become possible.

First we should note that the Hassania in the cotton-picking season move to settle on their hawashas (farms). The nuzal pickers have straw huts built for them by their employer, and they settle on the same farm site with him and his family. The nuzal always take their families with them to the farm so that they all can earn money by cotton-picking. On the farm site, sedentary and pastoral families interact directly with each other, and members of the two families come to know each other very well--especially the womenfolk. General exchanges of fire, firewood, water, and occasionally food take place, starting in a limited way and gradually increasing if the contractual relationship extends over some years.

We have seen an illustration of a high degree of interaction between two families who have come to know each other only through this dyadic contractual relationship. The two families interact on a semi-classificatory kinship basis by assuming the obligation to reciprocate and exchange visits and gifts on such occasions as death or marriage. Thus the interaction on the farm site has later been extended to a wider network of relationships.

We have seen from the case given that this extended social interaction may go on even after the contractual relationship has ended. The now fully integrated nomad acts as a broker or agent for the former sedentary employer. Thus in the case of Mohammed Ali he was able to get a new employee through his former employee. Moreover, it is very likely that a new employee will be a close relative of the old one, and so the sedentary family will be interacting with virtually the same group of closely related kin, which gives some continuity to the social interaction in spite of the change in personnel.

But has this socio-economic interaction resulted in any tendency toward assimilation or sedentarization rather than incorporation of additional nomads?

There are very few cases of intermarriage between nomads and sedentary people (see Table 4). Lineage endogamy is the prevailing rule among the riverain Arabs, and the outside marriages that occur are almost always made with other sedentary people rather than with nomads. Also, there are very few cases in the Sufi village where nomads have come with their families and permanently settled there.

However, Table 1 shows that some nomads appear on the labor force lists even during the early agricultural activities such as dura and cotton clearance. In spite of the peak demand for their labor at home (this is the kharif season), they have chosen to seek cash in the schemes. Sedentarization may follow in such cases--especially if these people have to move to and fro with their families frequently. But this is only a possibility, not a certainty.

Table 4

MARRIAGES OF MALES IN FOUR GENERATIONS AMONG THE GARNAB SECTION OF THE AMRIA/HASSANIA LINEAGE AT SUFI VILLAGE

Generation (Eldest = 4)	In-Group Marriages	Outside Marriages: Marriages with Sedentary People	Outside Marriages: Marriages with Nomads
4	5	1	--
3	9	6	1
2	22	12	2
1	109	6	2

Conclusion

The employment of pastoral nomads in cotton-picking in a sedentary context has resulted in a high degree of economic interdependence between pastoral economy and sedentary cultivation. A pattern of socio-economic interaction has developed and become a characteristic feature of nomadic/sedentary relations. Mutual need, trust, and goodwill are the emerging principles, and the model of mutual hostility between nomads and their sedentary neighbors becomes a myth. Both nomads and sedentary people place high value on their economic interdependence because through this process not only is each contributing to the economy of the other, but each is also contributing to the continuity of his own system. Data relating to intermarriage between the two groups and other possible ways in which nomads could have been sedentarized lead one to conclude that while each group values economic interdependence, each prefers its own way of life. This seems to confirm I.M. Lewis's claim that "nomads prefer the devil they know to the devil they do not know."[9] However, a key implication of the preceding analysis is that sedentary life for nomads is no longer a devil they do not know! Why then do they set a limit to their socio-economic interaction? Or has the limit been set by the sedentary people, or by both groups?

It is difficult to answer this question, and one can only draw attention to the time factor involved. The participation of nomads in cotton-picking was not really considerable until the mid-1950's, though it started much earlier. Now that economic and social interaction has taken place, is it not possible that a sedentarization process may follow?

Footnotes

[1]I.M. Lewis, "Nomadism: An Anthropological View." FAO conference paper (Cairo, December 1971), p. 2. [My emphasis.]

[2]*Ibid.*, p. 1.

[3]Nader Afshar Nadevi, "The Settlement of Nomads, and Its Social and Economic Implications." FAO conference paper (Cairo, 1971).

[4]Altogether these nomadic groups make up about one-fifth of the total population of the Dar.

[5]Lewis.

[6]The role of Mahdism in bringing nomads and sedentary folk together is very similar to the Sanusiya role in Cyrenaica in

bringing bedu and hadr together (E. Evans-Pritchard, The Sanusi of Cyrenaica [Oxford: Oxford University Press, 1949]).

[7]This computation is very rough because there is no guarantee that the 41 cases make a representative sample: the sample constitutes about 10 percent of the total number of farm plots in the scheme. As for the money actually spent on cotton-picking, the farmers have given figures suggesting that the scheme loans are wholly spent.

[8]Talal Asad, The Kababish Arabs: Power, Authority and Consent in a Nomadic Tribe (London: C. Hurst and Co., 1970).

[9]Lewis.

THE ENMESHMENT OF NOMADS IN SA'UDI ARABIAN SOCIETY: THE CASE OF ĀL MURRAH

Donald P. Cole

Introduction

Most anthropological research concerning nomads has been carried out in areas where there are high degrees of ethnic plurality. The nomads themselves, often claiming different historical origins, speaking different languages, and maintaining strong notions of cultural separateness, are major contributors to the ethnic diversity, both among themselves and vis-à-vis the sedentary population. Consequently, their involvement with the greater society is often seen as occurring indirectly in the political and economic spheres rather than as being fully participant in a common culture and social system that embraces both sedentary and nomadic components.

In Sa'udi Arabia, however, cultural unity between pastoral nomads, or Bedouins, and the majority of the sedentary population is very strong. Throughout Najd, the desert-steppe homeland of the Al Sa'ud and the central region of the contemporary Kingdom of Sa'udi Arabia, as well as in most of the Eastern Province of Al Hasa and in much of the Hejaz, there is a strong cultural identity between nomads and sedentary villagers and urbanites. Only in the mountainous areas of the Asir, where there is perhaps a close cultural tie with highland Yemen, in the major cities of the Hejaz with their large ajnabi (foreign) populations, and in some oasis and fishing villages in the Eastern Province, where some have strong identities as sha'ab al-khalij (people of the Gulf), are there strong feelings of cultural separateness, usually tinged by religious differences. Nevertheless, all but the ajnabi Hejazis, ex-African slaves, and a few recent immigrants are Arabs, and type of activity and genealogy rather than ethnic origin are the major criteria for social differentiation that group people

---

The research upon which this paper is based was carried out as part of the requirements for a Ph.D. degree in Anthropology at the University of California, Berkeley. During 1968-70, the author spent eighteen months with the Āl Murrah nomads and six months in Riyadh, Taif, Dammam, and other cities. The research was financed by a grant from the National Institute of Mental Health, for which the author is most grateful.

into a number of categories which, in certain situations, cut across even nomad-sedentary boundaries.

Partially as a result of ecology, which requires "horizontal" rather than "vertical" nomadism, or transhumance, both nomadic and sedentary people are enmeshed together in a complex network of social, economic, and political relationships, and share a common ongoing cultural tradition. I suggest that it is misleading to think of Sa'udi Arabian nomads as making up "part-societies, part-cultures," for such a conceptualization implies a kind of static wholeness, or closed system, that is not present. Even the Āl Murrah, probably the most highly mobile camel nomads in Sa'udi Arabia, are so highly integrated into urban-based Sa'udi Arabian society, both to meet a vast number of their economic, social, and cultural needs and as a military-political force to serve as the backbone of both the founding and the maintenance of the present-day nation-state, that it is impossible to conceive of them as a separate unit.

In this paper I am concerned to show how this integration, or enmeshment, occurs at three different levels--each one of which utilizes different social units. At the first level the focus is on the ways in which villages fit into the ecology of pastoral nomadism; a lineage-type structure is the unit of social organization most operative at this level. At the second level the focus is on the ways in which a tribe, taken as a unit in itself, is tied to a regional urban center which is the locus of many activities necessary to the life of the nomad, as well as the major field of activity of successful tribal leaders. At the third level the focus is on the way in which tribes, taken together as a single category in Sa'udi Arabian society, provide the military foundation of the nation-state.

The view I present is limited, however, because I have elected to discuss only a few basic aspects of the nomads' enmeshment in the wider society, and have more or less ignored the sedentary population. Furthermore, since the Āl Murrah are a highly mobile and isolated group, they do not display all the patterns of integration used by nomads in Sa'udi Arabia. However, some of the basic principles that underlie the nomads' enmeshment are present in the Āl Murrah social organization and are part of their cultural perceptions, and as such provide material that will illuminate the basic processes at work in Sa'udi Arabian society.

Horizontal Nomadism and Oasis Villages

The Āl Murrah are exceptional among Sa'udi Arabian nomads in that the greater part of their tribal territory, located in the Rub' al-Khālī, is devoid of permanently settled agricultural communities. Nevertheless, the pattern of nomadism they follow is basically similar to that followed by other pastoralists in Sa'udi Arabia, and their exploitation of four semi-settled date palm oases resembles the pattern of agricultural development within tribal territories in general.

The area known as dirat al-Murrah (Murrah territories) is composed of a number of designated geographic areas and is occupied exclusively by the Āl Murrah, although other pastoralists, like the Āl Murrah outside their own territory, have the right--on a temporary, transient basis only--to pass through and drink from Āl Murrah wells. The Āl Murrah themselves normally leave this area during the winter and spring to graze areas outside their territory. All of their wells, however, are located within their tribal territory, and they return to these each summer for the gaidh (summer camp). Each major well or group of small wells is typically the property of a fakhd, or maximal lineage, and the group that camps together each summer corresponds very closely, although seldom exactly, with the members of a single lineage.

During the rest of the year, the lineage breaks up into groupings of from one to usually no more than four independent household-herding units which migrate in search of good pasturage. Although they normally leave their own territory for winter pasturage, this does not involve any large-scale group migration, and they do not have to cross hostile or non-tribal territories even though they may travel, in some years, as far as 1000 kilometers before reaching a desirable winter pasture area. Consequently, there is no need for them to obtain special rights of passage from any local population. Nor do they need the leadership of any kind of headmen or arbitration by any other group of people. Winter pastures are determined by the state of the grazing, and may be shared with any number of other tribal groups so long as the pasturage is sufficient to support all comers.

So far as pasturage is concerned, the summer is by far the most difficult time for the Āl Murrah and most other Sa'udi Arabian pastoralists. Unlike the Berbers in North Africa and most Iranian groups, they do not have cool mountain valleys or highland pastures to graze. Grasses and shrubs are likely to be in short supply, and over-grazing of the areas immediately around the major wells is common, since the herds must stay near sources of water because of their increased need for liquid during the hot summer. Consequently, the existence of agriculture--mainly in the form of date palms--is a very welcome adjunct to the summer wells. The palm groves provide not only a pleasant escape from the heat, but also dates for human consumption during times of plenty and for the feeding of camels during times of drought. There is also bersim (alfalfa), which is a useful supplement to the diets of sheep and goats, in particular.

The Āl Murrah possess only four such oases, and most of the herding groups camp alone at wells in the Rub' al-Khālī. None of the four Āl Murrah oases now supports a permanently settled population. Other tribes, however, occupy more fertile areas with better water resources, and consequently have oases which are permanently settled by kindred claiming similar tribal descent to the nomads. These oases are also used as nomad summer camps.

In much of the Wadi 'Ajman in northeastern Sa'udi Arabia, a number of villages have recently been developed, and agriculture has been expanded and improved through the development of deep wells. Probably a majority of the leading families of the Āl 'Ajman have built houses for themselves near their lineage-owned wells. Although these houses are often occupied only during the summer months, they nevertheless represent the increasing importance of agriculture and settlements in the life of this Bedouin tribe.

A much older settled area is the Wadi Dawasir in southern Najd, in which (according to Āl Murrah informants) whole lineages long ago settled in agricultural villages and abandoned nomadism. Known as hadhara min al-gadiim, they are considered, by the Āl Murrah at least, to be members--along with the Ad Dawasir nomads--of the Ad Dawasir tribe, although possibly of a slightly lower status than the nomads, whom the Āl Murrah nomads are more likely to identify with and to know personally. The few Ad Dawasir nomads I met considered themselves better off than the Āl Murrah because they were able to utilize their kinsmen's oases during the summer and claim a right to a proportion of the date harvest. Many of these nomads own palm trees which are taken care of by the settled people; in return, the nomads often take care of animals owned by the villagers.

The Bani Sa'id occupy a string of villages across central Najd, from near Riyadh to Taif. They claim membership in the 'Ataybah tribe, within whose tribal territory their villages are located, although they supposedly once were members of the Qahtan tribe before the Qahtan lost control of the area to the 'Ataybah. This change in tribal affiliation reflects two important aspects of tribalism in Sa'udi Arabia. The first is that, although genealogies are quoted in terms of descent, affiliation ultimately rests on the actions of a group, which largely determine its status. Whole lineages, for example, sometimes change tribal affiliation while other lineages change from subservient status to equal status if they begin to act like free and independent tribesmen. The second aspect is that tribal affiliation places a group in a certain status in Sa'udi Arabian society. That the Bani Sa'id are members of the 'Ataybah tribe means that they are 'asil (pure) and thus not of subservient status. That there is some doubt, however, about their actual descent from 'Ataybah suggests that they may not be quite the equals of their nomadic brethren, who represent the general cultural ideal of the pure, free Arab--the implication being that the Bani Sa'id accepted affiliation in the conquering tribe rather than nobly suffering defeat along with their displaced former relatives.

While both the Ad Dawasir and Bani Sa'id settlements probably represent very ancient establishments, both the Āl 'Ajman settlements and the Āl Murrah attempts at settlements are phenomena of this century and are related to both the pre- and post-oil periods in Sa'udi Arabia. All the Āl Murrah attempts at settlement, at least twice at Jabrin and once at Al-Khinn, As-sikak, and Nibak, were organized under the influence of a religious revival movement that swept through Sa'udi Arabia during the first decades of this century. Banding together as the Ikhwān al-Muslimīn (Muslim Brotherhood), many nomads, including parts of the Āl 'Ajman, Ad Dawasir, 'Ataybah, and almost all the other major Sa'udi tribes, attempted to establish hujār (settlements) where they could live and be ready for immediate call to participation in any jihad, and where they could more perfectly tend to their religious duties as true Muslims. In this, they followed the leadership of several tribal shaikhs, such as Faisal Ibn Duwish of the Mutayr tribe, who established a famous and powerful community at Al-Artawiya in the Mutayr tribal territory in northeastern Sa'udi Arabia, and of elements of the sedentary elite, such as 'Abd al-Aziz Ibn Sa'ud, who rode to power along with the Ikhwān movement.

The purposes of these settlements were determined by religious zeal, since it was thought that nomadism made it very difficult, if not impossible, for one to be a proper Muslim. Consequently, those who attempted sedentarization did so not in response to any economic forces or motivations, but in order to be able to study and know the Holy Quran and the Hadith of the Prophet, to be able to adhere strictly to the rituals of Islam, and to provide a ready standing army of Mujahidīn (holy warriors). Many of these settlements, including those of the Āl Murrah, failed, however, as major ongoing settlements--not because of any lack of religious zeal, but because the settlers could not support themselves by their primitive and half-hearted attempts at agriculture alone. Eventually these Āl Murrah (and many of the other Muslim Brothers) had to revert to the desert and pastoralism in order to subsist.

Recently, the benefits of income derived from oil have made many of the old Ikhwān settlements, along with new ones, spring to life as modern wells tap deep underground sources of water. In many instances, government projects are responsible for this new development--especially the major infrastructural changes. Many of the young men of the tribes also contribute to the development of these oases by sending back most of their wages earned in jobs in the developing urban areas of Arabia or in oil camps, or for their services in the various National Guards of the area. These newly developed oases fit well into a changed pastoral economy which is tending to concentrate on sheep and goats produced primarily for urban markets rather than on camels or sheep and goats produced primarily for subsistence. In the new herding patterns, trucks play a central role, and settlements that can provide gasoline and oil supplies are very important.

In both the older Ikhwān settlements and the newer ones, the social unit which predominates is the fakhd, or maximal lineage. Each of the Āl Murrah oases is the domain of a single lineage except Jabrin, where several closely related lineages from the same subtribe--the Āl Jaber--have each settled in separate areas of the oasis. Leadership in each place is vested in a member of the leading family who founded the Ikhwān settlement and who is known as <u>amir al-hijra</u>. Two of these families are from two of the three shaikhly lineages of the Āl Murrah, although the current paramount shaikh of the Āl Murrah and his lineage have so far refused to participate in any settlement scheme. The other two amir al-hijra families rose to preeminence through activities associated with the Ikhwān. Nowadays, each of these extended families has some members who follow a purely nomadic existence, some who divide their time between nomadism and such things as politics, work in urban areas, or retainership in princely courts, and some who remain in the household of the <u>amir</u>, who does not migrate with the rest of his lineage but stays near the oasis throughout the year.

During the period of the Ikhwān movement, in each of these places large mudbrick castles were built which were inhabited by the leading families. Most of these have now fallen into partial or complete disuse. During the last five or six years, however, each place has been experiencing a considerable upsurge in activity as it becomes an important summer gathering place both for the nomads and for lineage members who have gone away to work and who return to spend summer vacations with their kinsmen. An increasing amount of building, both of mudbrick and palm-frond thatching, is occurring, with the most typical buildings consisting of sitting rooms with coffee hearths for the men and separate kitchens and rooms for the women. Most of these new buildings, erected mainly for comfort and hospitality, are built by hired laborers--mainly Yemenis--at the expense of families who have sons working in Kuwait, Qatar, or other parts of Sa'udi Arabia.

These new houses are not erected by "nouveau riche"-type families. On the contrary, all the still-living old men of these families were highly distinguished tribal raiders and/or Ikhwān warriors. Furthermore, all of them own very find herds of purebred milk and riding camels, a sign of well-being in the pre-oil economy. A great deal of feasting and socializing goes on at all these houses during the summer months as each family seeks to maintain or enhance its position through the generosity of its coffee hearth and the feasts it provides. Consequently, a slight differentiation in status is beginning to develop as the less wealthy families stay in their tents throughout the summer (although they camp in the oasis at least during the date harvest). Some of these less wealthy families are beginning to build small huts for themselves, but they seldom attempt to compete with the hospitality of the riajīl al-kibār ("big men") of their lineages. In the desert, however, the hospitality of all is equal; it is only within the settlements that any kind of differentiation begins to appear.

Consequently, when we look at even a semi-settled oasis such as any of those of the Āl Murrah, it is possible to see at least three, and possibly four, distinctly emergent statuses. Three of them--the "big men" and the shaikhs, the average tribesmen who partially settle but do not compete in hospitality with their more fortunate lineage mates, and the nomads who camp at wells in the desert and do not participate in oasis life at all--are united by similar tribal affiliation, and within the tribal ideology are all of equal status. This egalitarian ideology of the tribe reflects, however, only the social organization of the nomads in the desert, where each herding unit is free and independent and is bound to other herding units only through considerations of kinship and marriage or neighborliness. Within the settlements, status differentiation begins to become apparent even among tribal members.

Outside, non-tribal forces play an important part in this status differentiation. All the leading men are such because of their past exploits in extra-tribal affairs, mainly as members of the Ikhwān or in other fighting that led to the establishment of the Kingdom of Sa'udi Arabia. As a result, they have important urban contacts. Many of the purely nomadic families have equally brilliant pasts and equally important urban contacts with people in the government and the royal family, but because of their strict adherence to nomadism, many of them fail to utilize these contacts and are possibly beginning to slip in their overall position, although they are still highly respected if considered a bit "old fashioned." The average tribesmen who settle fall behind both groups because they fail to compete in hospitality with other people in the settlement and often lack any important urban contacts which could lead to good jobs or help them secure a position in the military.

A fourth status, about which there is no question of differentiation, is that of hired laborers. Few of the nomads who are now settling do any of the hard labor involved in either building houses or agriculture. Nomads often work very hard with their hands, digging out wells and tending palm trees if they have to. However, the increased wealth of the region that has made possible the new settlements has also provided the nomads with money to hire laborers. The laborers are all considered outsiders, and most come from the Yemen, Oman, or Iraq, and are thus not even Sa'udi Arabians. Furthermore, much of the modernized, market-oriented sheep and goat herding is done by foreign nomads or members of subservient tribes for pay, rather than by the owners or their families, who are thus freed to pursue activities in urban areas at the same time that they keep their tents with their herds operating in the desert. It is perhaps too early to see if the laborers will become permanent members in the communities in which they are now working. Many of the Āl Jaber at Jabrin, for example, expressed a negative reaction to government plans to develop their oasis because of fears that this would bring in a permanent group of lower status workers and market people. They preferred Jabrin to remain undeveloped but united in overall tribal structure without drastic differences in status.

If we can take these examples as representing the basic ways in which many Sa'udi Arabian villages have developed, or at least as providing us with models of the ways in which nomads are related to villages within their tribal territories, we see that the nomad-sedentary boundary is not a precise one--at least in a social sense. Nomads are intimately involved with their villages, particularly at the lineage level, because they camp at them during the summer and because some lineage members settle at the site of their lineage's summer camp, allowing them to have relatively close contact with each other. Furthermore, both nomad and village settler identify themselves as of tribal origin, and though slight status-differentiation may develop between them through different patterns of hospitality and different access to urban centers of power and wealth, they are nevertheless united in their differentiation from hired laborers and any others they cannot relate to on a tribal basis, including ex-slaves and many lower class urban people whom they have no special social relationship with.

Nomadic Tribes and Regional Urban Centers

While I have suggested that village settlements in tribal territories are most likely to correspond to and interact mainly with nomads at the subtribal grouping of the lineage, a nomadic tribe, as a grouping in itself, is most likely to be involved with a regional urban center, such as the major market and administrative city of an oasis. We have already noted that the leading men of the developing tribal settlements, as well as of the purely nomadic groups, rely on contacts in urban centers for much of their preeminence. These contacts are primarily on a national or even international level within the Arabian peninsula, but at least for the shaikhs of the tribe this includes a regional urban center with which the tribe has traditional relationships and of which it is likely to be considered a member body.

[Although this is a subject for a paper in itself, at this point I should like to briefly adumbrate the kinds of relationships that tribal groups maintain with regional urban centers. That these relationships are considered to be from al-gadīm (olden times) and not just recent developments that are part of the development of the nation-state, suggests that their integration into a more complex society beyond the level of the segmentary tribe is very basic to their way of life.

[Many of the major traditional cities of Sa'udi Arabia are very closely associated with the major tribe in whose territory they are located. Hail, for example, is known as balad as-Shammar (a Shammar town). A major part of the settled population there claims descent from different segments of the Shammar, and prior to the Al Sa'ud conquest, the rulers of Hail were the Al Rashīd, who were from a shaikhly lineage of the Shammar. Another example is Khaibar in the northern Hejaz, which is the earliest known center of the 'Anazah tribe and whose two sections are called Bishr and Ijlas, names which denote the two major divisions of the 'Anazah.

[The Āl Murrah claim a special relationship with Najran, in southwestern Sa'udi Arabia, and say that it is their home town. They claim to have traditional rights there, and say that one side of the market area of Najran belongs to them; thus, no non-Murrah can legally establish themselves there. Although the Āl Murrah have increasingly focused their urban activities on the Al Hasa oasis in eastern Arabia since at least the middle of the nineteenth century, they still have close social and political relationships with various tribal elements (both sedentary and nomadic) in the population of Najran, with whom they also share a common dialect. The Āl Murrah claimed that Najran was part of Sa'udi Arabia rather than of the Yemen because of their role as a member community within its populace. Mainly because of their concern for their tribal relatives, with whom they unite as the Āl Yam, the Āl Murrah participated in a jihad under the general leadership of the Al Sa'ud to put down their traditional enemies in the area--the Dahm tribes of the south. As a result, Najran was incorporated into Sa'udi Arabia in 1932.

[Most of the urban activities of the Āl Murrah are centered nowadays in the town of Hofuf, the capital of Al Hasa oasis, and they consider other Sa'udi Arabian cities, such as Riyadh, Taif, Jeddah, etc., to be outside their own dirah (homeland). Their involvement in Al Hasa is primarily economic and political rather than social because, unlike in Najran, they have no tribal relatives settled in the oasis. Their involvement there is directly related to the rise to power in the nineteenth century of the extended family of the present-day paramount shaikh of the Āl Murrah: Ibn Shoraim. Previously, the paramount shaikhs of the Āl Murrah operated in and out of Najran.]

Intertribal warfare in the Al Hasa area was an important feature in the Shoraim family's rise to preeminence. The Āl Murrah claim to have only recently established themselves through military conquest in this area, which was previously inhabited by other tribes. The Āl Shoraim and other members of their lineage were particularly involved in these exploits, and once they had undisputed control (or at least free access) to major sections of the desert around Al Hasa, they were in a position to make their influence felt in the administrative center of Hofuf. The Āl Murrah use the term as-siyasiya (diplomacy) to describe the activities their leaders carried out with the rulers of Al Hasa, at that time the Ottoman Turks, who offered them the governorship of the oasis at one time. Thus the ability to successfully interact in urban political circles is a major criterion of tribal leadership, for in this instance the former shaikhs of the Āl Murrah lost their preeminence in the tribe because of their refusal to interact with the governmental forces in Hofuf.

While nomadic tribal elites sometimes controlled important urban centers such as Hail in the past, the rulers of these major centers are now almost always members of the Al Sa'ud royal family, whom the Āl Murrah recognize as forming a special class of hakims (rulers). While the Al Sa'ud, alone among present-day Arab kings, do not claim sharif status through descent from the Prophet but through descent from a shaikhly section of the 'Anazah tribe, they are not properly equated with any of the tribal shaikhs of today, although both have equally good genealogies. Tribal shaikhs are not of hakim status, and thus do not concern themselves with basing their power on control of an urban following. However, the following they are able to command within their own tribe rests to a very great degree on their urban activities on behalf of the tribe rather than on their activities connected with nomadism.

That the power of shaikhs is related to their success in representing their tribes in urban circles is not so much due to their being middlemen who act as mediators between the two distinct groups, but rather is symbolic of the ways in which nomads are dependent on services that can be obtained only from specialists who almost always tend to reside in cities. Although most nomadic families are capable of self-sufficiency with regard to food, there are many needs basic to their cultural, social, and physical existence which can only be satisfied in the city. The Āl Murrah are seldom capable of performing anything for themselves other than activities directly related to herding. They rely on the cities for most of the equipment used in herding, for a myriad of religious services that includes circumcision, special cures for both physical and psychological ailments, marriage approvals, and the settlement of contested divorces or marriage separations, for many legal procedures used in conflict resolution, and for the procurement of the coffee, tea, sugar, and cardamom that are essential to their socializing--not to mention a number of the staples of their diet. Furthermore, as Muslims, they must pay their zakat tax to the hakim of the city to which their tribe is most closely attached.

Thus, even nomads from the Rub' al-Khālī maintain relationships with numerous people in the city. Their shaikh is concerned to protect their interests in all the different aspects of their involvement with the city, but he specializes particularly in dealing with conflict resolution procedures which involve both governmental and religious officials.

The pattern of interaction between the nomads and the urban-based governmental and Islamic authorities is not one of a central government attempting to encapsulate a potentially recalcitrant tribe that is autonomous and capable of providing all its own needs and dealing with all its own conflicts. On the contrary, the nomads are dependent on many specialists in the urban areas--including members of the royal family, whom they treat not so much like royalty as like highly respected tribal shaikhs (as when they say that Faisal bin 'Abd al-Aziz--not King Faisal--is indeed a great shaikh, or that they are Āl Murrah Āl Faisal--People of Murrah of the People of Faisal).

Tribes as a National Military Force

One other way in which the major nomadic tribes are integrally a part of Sa'udi Arabian society is as a military force that was operative at the time of the founding of the present Sa'udi kingdom and still provides the major military support of the nation-state. This military activity is considered by the nomads to be their major speciality within the community of Islam--an ideology with which the nation-state of Sa'udi Arabia is intimately involved. It is significant that both the Sanusi in Cyrenaica and the Al Sa'ud and the Al 'Abd al-Wahab in Najd appealed to the nomads to participate in their major religio-political undertakings as holy warriors. Evans-Pritchard's description of the Cyrenaican Bedouins' participation in Islam is particularly relevant:

> Although they are negligent Muslims themselves they respect piety in others. Brothers of the Sanusiya Order and religious men in general ought to pray regularly. That is their business

> and it is very necessary for the well-being of the community and worthy of liberal support, but the Bedouin is an unlettered man, a shepherd and a warrior, and he has his own affairs to see to. . . . [T]he Bedouin make up for their shortcomings by their enthusiasm for the _jihad_, holy war against unbelievers.[1]

What seems most significant in this statement is not that Bedouins are "negligent Muslims" because they do not pray regularly, but that the society is organized in such a way that there are religious specialists upon whose existence the well-being of the society depends, along with other specialists: warriors, shepherds, agriculturalists, merchants, bureaucrats. Each has his own affairs to tend to, but they all work together and use each other's specialities. Furthermore, they are not foreigners to each other. Evans-Pritchard places too much stress on the ways in which the _'alim_ who came from the west and taught the beliefs and law of Islam to Cyrenaican Bedouins was basically different from them: "He could arbitrate among them because he was not of them. He was not, like them, a tented son of the steppe, though his descendants may have learned to live as such, but a _Marabat_, a man who follows religion and not the rains."[2] While Sa'udi Arabian hakims and shaikhs of Islam are also different from the Bedouin of Sa'udi Arabia, all groups must work together within a single system of rules that is understood and accepted by all. Otherwise, how could the marabat or the hakim act effectively as arbitrators in a society to which they were total outsiders?

Still inspired by Wahaby preaching, Sa'udi Arabian nomads are perhaps not so negligent in their duties as Muslims as the Cyrenaican, but they do not consider themselves capable of giving authoritative interpretations of the religion. They do, however, have a conception of themselves as _Mujahidīn_ (holy warriors), and much of the activity of all the major nomadic tribes is related to warfare. [The important military role they played in the religious revival movement that resulted in the establishment of Sa'udi Arabia can only be noted in passing.] I shall briefly describe how they fit into the military structure of contemporary Sa'udi Arabia and suggest how this activity fits in with their overall social and economic existence, for many Sa'udi Arabian nomads depend heavily on their military activities for much of their subsistence.

What is probably by far the most effective military force in Sa'udi Arabia is the National Guard, which is composed almost exclusively of nomads. The Sa'udi Arabian Army, which has only recently been created, is composed mainly of non-tribal peoples from the Hejaz and falls under the bureaucratic administration of the Ministry of Defense and Aviation. The National Guard, however--at least in 1968-70--was under the personal command of a brother of the King and was independent from any of the national bureaucratic ministries. Generally speaking, the National Guard has evolved from the old Ikhwān al-Muslimīn armies which once attempted to settle in oases in their own tribal territories. At present, however, full-time members of the National Guard, selected on a tribal basis, are stationed in camps that are usually located just outside the main cities of the kingdom. The groups that are on full-time duty appear to come mainly from tribes that are not native to the particular area they are defending or guarding. Although the members of one unit may come mainly from one tribe, almost every unit has a few members from other tribes as well.

Some members of the Āl Murrah are in units of the National Guard, and some of the leading men who have recently settled in places like Jabrin have important positions in the Guard, but as a group the Āl Murrah are more involved in a reserve section of the National Guard that is commanded by their paramount shaikh, or amir, and which has its headquarters within the territory frequented by Āl Murrah nomads. These headquarters serve as a focal center for the whole tribe, and indeed attendance at guard meetings is the only major activity which serves to unite the tribesmen. Without this activity, there would seldom be any reason for many of the lineages of the Āl Murrah ever to come in contact with each other.

No one is automatically a member of the National Guard, and not all households have members in it. The lineages that are most closely related to the shaikh of the Āl Murrah have a larger proportion of their members enrolled in the Guard than any of the others, although every lineage is represented. None of the members of the other two shaikhly lineages of the Āl Murrah participate in this reserve unit of the National Guard, although a few of their members are attached to other units--but not as commanders. At the headquarters, each lineage has a room or several contiguous rooms reserved for it. All of the lineage mates eat their meals together communally, and have their own coffee and tea hearths. Each group has a commander who is usually from its own lineage and who reports to the amir in a special council. The amir has assistants, who include his sons, his father's brother's sons, and a number of other men who are close relatives.

Although the living arrangements in the camp tend to follow kinship groupings, at the one time I was able to observe them engaged in practice exercises the units that operated together on active guard duty were mixed between five or six different lineages, and each lineage was likely to have its members spread throughout the province rather than together. In the absence of warfare, the only activity the reserve unit usually has to perform is monthly attendance at the headquarters to receive their salaries, which amount to about $100 per month for an average member.

This income is used to buy products in the market at Hofuf, although deductions are made from it to cover any expenses that the lineages as a whole might have. If, for example, the lineage decides to modernize any of its wells, a tax will be made on the salaries of all of the lineage members who are in the National Guard. Those household-herding units who have no members in the Guard pay nothing, but have equal rights in using the wells. Also, blood money and money for other damages is collected from these salaries, being divided according to the number of individual members in the Guard rather than according to individual households.

Although no members of the Āl Murrah were on active duty during the period I lived with them, they were always on call, and during the previous year they had been on active duty in Najran because of the Egyptian-backed Yemeni attacks against Sa'udi Arabia in that area. Most of the major Sa'udi Arabian tribes regularly send many of their members to active duty in units of the National Guard.

It might well be asked how these herdsmen can spare a high percentage of their young men to be away and involved in military activities on even a semi-permanent basis. In almost all the herding units of the Āl Murrah, there are more men than are needed to carry out the herding activities even of camels, which require much more attention than do sheep and goats. Consequently, almost every unit can easily spare at least one or two members for military duties. This seems to be no different from the past; the unit of the Āl Murrah I traveled with carried on the same kinds of camel-herding activities that must have been traditional for a very long time. Even in the past, when the Āl Murrah had fewer of the amenities of modern life, most of their young men were away on war parties or raids, as most of the old men of the tribe can attest.

The additional income is extremely important to the average household, and the centralizing function provided by the National Guard unit serves to keep the tribe united and in close contact, instead of each group following its own special migratory patterns. Thus, instead of attempting to destroy tribal unity, the national government of Sa'udi Arabia through the structure of the National Guard provides a mechanism for maintaining tribal unity at the same time that it incorporates the tribes into its own power structure.

Within a developing Sa'udi Arabia, the National Guard provides young nomads with an opportunity to learn new skills and to participate in the national society in a way that is acceptable to them. They are neither so inclined nor does their present level of education allow a significant number of them to work as administrators in the government or take positions in modern business activities other than those of laborers or drivers. The Guard also provides a means of increasing the purchasing power of the tribes, at the same time making them feel that they are an integral part of a developing Sa'udi Arabia. Generally speaking, the loyalty of the tribes to the Al Sa'ud and the type of monarchy based on Islamic principles that they represent seems unquestioned. Thus the basic military support they provide the regime and the country as a whole is obvious, although possibly resented by some of the modernizing middle class, who have little understanding of the traditional social structure of Arabia, which is still very relevant to many aspects of life in the area.

Conclusion

I have presented a general discussion of three ways in which Sa'udi Arabian nomads and sedentaries are integrated in a complex network of social relationships in which various types of social units are utilized in various types of situations. I have suggested that we think of the nomads and sedentaries as *enmeshed* in a single system rather than as discrete, well-bounded units. The situation is much more complex than I have described, because I have ignored differences between nomadic groups and have only briefly referred to differentiation in the sedentary components. The tribe I know best is a very isolated one, but even it is so involved in the wider society that it cannot be properly understood without reference to the larger group.

As anthropologists I think we too often attempt to see whatever social group we are concerned with as being a well-defined and bounded social unit. We are particularly guilty of this when dealing with the Middle East. Murphy and Kasdan, for example, speak of "Arab Bedouin society" as if it were some kind of clearly demarcated and bounded unit of social organization that can stand on its own in comparison with societies such as the Nuer or Zuñi.[3] Because of this point of view, they feel justified in seeing Arab Bedouin society as implicitly different from Arab peasant society[4] and in contrast to central state societies (". . . for Bedouin society persists today amid the ruins of empires that once sought to shatter it").[5] As I have attempted to show briefly in this paper and more fully elsewhere,[6] such a division obscures the dynamics of Middle Eastern society. A more effective approach would focus on regions and the nation itself as major fields of social activity rather than on purely local or tribal groupings, which, though they may claim exclusiveness, are intimately involved in and affected by the wider society.

Footnotes

[1]E.E. Evans-Pritchard, The Sanusi of Cyrenaica (Oxford: Clarendon Press, 1949), p. 63.

[2]Ibid., p. 68.

[3]Robert Murphy and Leonard Kasdan, "The Structure of Parallel Cousin Marriage," American Anthropologist, 61 (1959), pp. 17-29.

[4]Ibid., p. 28n.

[5]Ibid., p. 27.

[6]Donald P. Cole, "The Social and Economic Structure of the Al Murrah: A Saudi Arabian Bedouin Tribe" (Ph.D. dissertation, University of California, Berkeley, 1971).

THE ENCAPSULATION OF NOMADIC SOCIETIES IN IRAN

G. Reza Fazel

There is little doubt that nomadic populations in the Middle East are being deeply affected by recent modernizing processes. Judging by the evidence of the last few decades, it is reasonable to assume that sooner or later all nomadic societies in the Middle East will have to undergo fundamental restructuring in adjusting to their rapidly changing social and physical environment.

In my view, the question before us is not whether change is inevitable, but rather the nature of the modes of articulation and accommodation between the nomadic peoples and the larger structures of which they are parts.

It is interesting that while some nomadic populations are changing or have changed--sometimes beyond recognition--either through sedentarization and subsequent detribalization or through absorption by sedentary communities, other groups have miraculously remained relatively unaffected. Why? To ignore this question by concentrating simply on the end-results of change would be to overlook the important processes whereby the nomadic and sedentary structures interact.

A useful analytical framework is that provided by F.G. Bailey as applied to the relationships between the Indian bureaucratic state structure and the "small-scale relatively undifferentiated tribal or village structures"--the konds of Orissa, for example.[1] Briefly, he maintains that "almost without exception today these structures exist within larger encapsulating political structures"--i.e., independent nation-states. These larger structures are, of course, much more complex and command much greater political resources than the smaller ones they enclose.

There are, according to Bailey, at least three possible ways in which the two structures interact:

> At one extreme is the situation in which the encapsulation is merely nominal, merely, one might say a matter of geography. The leaders of [the encapsulating structures] either cannot or choose not to interfere with [the encapsulated structure]. . . . They might not have the resources to interfere . . . or they might not consider it worth their

> while because the payoff for successful intervention might not exceed the cost of the intervention. . . . The second possible posture for the leaders of the [encapsulating structure] is the predatory one: they do not concern themselves with what goes on inside the [encapsulated structure] as long as the people who live [in] it pay the revenue. . . . The final posture is that in which the ruling power has taken the decision that [the encapsulated structure] must be integrated: which in practice means radical change, if not abolition. . . . This is the posture adopted by virtually all the developing nations: they seek with varying degrees of determination and success, to put an end to . . . tribalism or regionalism and to make a united nation.[2]

The basic assumption of this paper, especially in reference to the last "posture," is that the extent to which tribal structures in the Middle East (or more specifically, in Iran) are encapsulated varies according to certain conditions. These conditions are expressed here in terms of three variables: (1) ecologic circumstances vis-à-vis the sedentary populations, (2) the degree of integration into the national market economy, and (3) the degree of political compatibility between the state structures and their tribal enclaves.

The distinction of these variables is to facilitate analysis; it does not imply that they are absolutely discrete spheres of transaction. Ecologic relationships between nomads and sedentary populations include some activities which are purely economic, involving exchanges of goods and services, and a relationship between ecologic conditions and political organization has been postulated by Barth in his study of the Basseri nomads of South Persia.[3]

I should like here to discuss the encapsulation processes among the Boyr Ahmad, focusing mainly on the three variables outlined above. Following this I shall attempt a comparative analysis of several relatively contiguous nomadic groups of south and southwest Iran, with special reference to the encapsulative forces and the circumstances under which they emerge.[4]

The Boyr Ahmad

Variable I: Ecologic Circumstances. The administrative district of Kuh Giluyeh and Boyr Ahmad in southwest Iran covers an area of some 15,000 sq. km. and has a total population of roughly 350,000, of which some 120,000 are Boyr Ahmad.[5] Geographically, it is bounded by the province of Fars to the east, the province of Khuzistan to the west, Bakhtiari and Isfahan to the north, and the oil fields of the Persian Gulf coast to the south. This region falls within the southwestern portion of the Zagros system, with its remarkable fold structures which are predominantly aligned from northwest to southeast in a distinctive pattern of elevated domes and imposing high peaks, such as the spectacular range of Kuh-e-Dena (14,500 ft.) near the northern margin. The structural disharmony between the drainage pattern and the major ranges has created a series of profound gorges, or tangs ("narrows"). The strategic disposition of these narrow, rocky defiles has played a significant role in the relative isolation of this region and in its defense against intruders. The Boyr Ahmad tribal territory can be divided into two distinct ecological zones: the high altitude valley belts (usually above 5000 ft.) and the low-lying foothills gradually merging with the dune landscape and barren salt flats of the Persian Gulf coast.

Except in the piedmont escarpment, summer pastures have a remarkably wide distribution, ranging from 5000 ft. to the 14,000 ft. terraces of Kuh-e-Dena. It is therefore not uncommon to find two summer pastures separated by as much as 100 kilometers. Frequently, the winter pasture of one group may serve as the summer quarters of another. Insofar as pasture utilization is concerned, the total picture is one of latitudinal distribution of the tribal segments rather than large-scale convergence and concentration at two widely separated summer and winter locations.

Based primarily on their modes of subsistence, the Boyr Ahmad population can be divided into three distinct but interdependent groups: the permanently settled agriculturalists; the nomadic sheep- and goat-herders who have a predominantly pastoral economy but do some subsidiary farming, mostly in their winter quarters; and the exclusively pastoral nomads. The last two groups occupy areas above 5000 ft. and comprise almost 90 percent of the population.

It would be misleading to regard the various forms of nomadism here as simply adaptive responses to the physical features of a dual zone. While the pastoral migration is a response to ecologic exigencies, migratory regimes are largely determined by the internal processes of coexistence among tribal sections, since practically all seasonal movements take place within the tribal territory.

Historically, the Boyr Ahmad have gone through several phases of expansion at the expense of the tribes along their boundaries. According to Fassai, 200 years ago the total territory of the core group did not exceed the oak-forested mountain belt to the north--some 20 miles wide and 60 miles long.[6] The acquisition of new territories made available much-needed winter pastures in the lowland areas. At the same time, rapid population growth--largely as a result of accretion and absorption of conquered peoples--resulted in a growing military superiority over neighboring tribes. Only within the last 45 years has a state of relative equilibrium been reached, and this is due mainly to the increasing influence of the central administration in the area.

Today, as probably 200 years ago, the Boyr Ahmad are completely surrounded by other tribal groups, including the Qashqai (Kashkuli and Farsi-Medan subtribes) to the north, Mamassani to the east, Bashte-Babui and Choram to the south, and Behmai, Taiyebi, Doshmanziari, and Zilai to the west. With the exception of the Turkic-speaking Qashqai, they all share fundamental features in terms of ethnic composition, language (Luri, a Farsi dialect), and economic and political organization. A complex and changing set of relationships between the Boyr Ahmad and each neighboring tribe has included marriage alliances (usually among the political leaders), exchanges involving pasture use, and economic transactions, mainly in grains and animals. However, this does not preclude competition for resources along the borders and sporadic clashes, especially with the Qashqai.

To sum up the important points thus far: (a) the Boyr Ahmad occupy a well-defined tribal territory with rich mountain pastures and arable lands, which are for the most part limited to valley floors and low-lying foothills, (b) the seasonal migrations of the pastoralist segments take place almost entirely within the tribal territory, and (c) a relatively stable relationship between the Boyr Ahmad and their tribal neighbors has been maintained through various boundary-maintaining mechanisms and through active administrative intervention for the last 45 years. For our present purposes, it should be emphasized that while inter- and intra-tribal competition for land and natural resources have not ceased completely, the absence of non-tribal sedentary populations has confined such competitive activities to groups who are on the whole ethnically, linguistically, economically, and culturally similar.

Variable II: The Degree of Economic Integration. The bohoon ("tent") is the basic social and economic unit among the Boyr Ahmad pastoralists. The economy of the tent-dwelling household is based on the ownership of three kinds of property: (1) a flock averaging 45 sheep and goats as productive capital and a number of transport animals, (2) movable property consisting of a tent, tools, and implements, and (3) land. Rights of access to pasture resources are determined by membership in the local descent group, or oulad.

It should be noted, however, that contrary to what has been suggested concerning the Basseri,[7] this nomad household is neither isolated nor independent economically, politically, or socially; it is tied to other households in the camping unit through a complex network of bonds and contractual relationships. In addition, the household as a unit of production and consumption has come increasingly to depend on a trade partner (doust: lit., a friend) for the purchase of certain products not produced by its members, such as tea, sugar, tobacco, utensils, cloth, etc., and the sale of its pastoral products--mainly clarified butter, wool, and male animals. The nomads also rely on town merchants for cash loans and credit to tide them over the recurrent slump periods, which leads in most cases to a state of perpetual indebtedness frequently passed on from one generation to the next.

Trade relations with the outside world began within the memory of my older informants--some 60-70 years ago. Although it is conceivable that the ruling elite, especially the khans, had some access to market towns, the bulk of market goods were acquired through raids on caravans which crossed the tribal land. Occasionally towns became the objects of organized raids, either mobilized or sanctioned by the paramount chief. The abandonment and subsequent ruin of at least one town now within the Boyr Ahmad territory is attributed to constant plundering by the khans.

The main commercial and administrative center for the entire region is the town of Behbahan to the south. However, the inconvenience of traveling long distances over rugged terrain makes frequent visits impractical. This, coupled with the predominantly seasonal nature of pastoral products (and hence credit availability), limits nomads' visits to Behbahan to once or twice a year. A substantial portion of market goods is therefore obtained through itinerant merchants--usually the trade partners noted above.

Two crucial factors for consideration here are land and labor. The amount of arable land available is limited. A recent increase in the amount of agricultural land has been at the expense of pasture resources. There is, however, no "land market" in this region to provide an alternative source of income for the wealthy nomads, as there is for the Basseri.[8] Purchase of land from the neighboring tribes, even if possible, would usually be undesirable for various social and political reasons--except as a form of self-imposed exile by a murderer or an unsuccessful political contender. It is safe to say that sedentarization is almost invariably achieved through the accumulation of wealth in animals within the tribe rather than through the purchase of land from outside.

Similarly, only a negligible number of herdless (usually as a result of successive losses of animals) tribesmen seek sources of income outside the tribe. This is due partly to the scarcity of employment opportunities in the towns and in other tribes, and partly to the existence of such opportunities within the Boyr Ahmad tribe itself. Economic differentiation in terms of unequal wealth in animals and agricultural land on the one hand, and labor requirements in connection with pastoral and agricultural activities on the other, have created multifarious contractual relationships between the wealthy and impoverished nomads, with important implications for the political structure and decision-making processes.

We may conclude then that, on the whole, in the dual economy of the Boyr Ahmad, transactions involving land and labor are not to any appreciable degree extended to the outside world, and therefore do not enter the sphere of market exchange. Therefore, no tribal land and very few labor opportunities are made available to outsiders--i.e., members of the neighboring tribes, and even less to townsmen.

Variable III: Political Organization. Structurally, the Boyr Ahmad are divided into six major sections or subtribes (tireh), each made up of a number of subsections (taifeh), which are in turn divided into a number of minor lineages (oulad). Oulads are further divided into several minimal lineages (tash) comprising a number of camping units. There are 3 to 10 tents (bohoon) in each camp. Subtribes are neither structurally equivalent nor genealogically related, though an extensive network of affinal ties serves to minimize conflict and foster good relations and solidarity, primarily among the contiguous groups. They differ chiefly in the size and number of their subdivisions. They also vary in terms of military power, wealth, and prestige, as well as genealogical tradition, and they enjoy varying degrees of independence and internal autonomy. Each section has one or more political leaders (kadkhoda), whose office is inherited through the male line.

The paramount chief, or khan (pl. khavanin), belongs to a distinct lineage, with no clearly established genealogical link to any particular subtribe. Khans represent the ideal values of the tribal life: honor, bravery, generosity, eloquence with a sense of humor, and above all, military power to counteract the divisive forces within the tribe. He is the symbolic embodiment of the political unity of the tribe, in which the autonomous subtribes and even their subdivisions are as much in competition with one another as with outsiders. As the supreme judge, the khan has the dual function of maintaining peace while at the same time preventing the formation of potentially dangerous coalitions among subtribes.

Nevertheless, more often than not, when a number of kadkhodas have not approved of a khan, they have plotted with his agnatic rivals and removed him by assassination or forced abdication. The weakening of an unpopular khan has sometimes been achieved through the delay or outright withholding of the annual levies and by subverting his armed body guards.

Externally, the relationship between the Boyr Ahmad and the central authorities has been long and not always harmonious. Administrative policies during the Safavid (1499-1722) and Qajar dynasties (1781-1925) tended toward regional and provincial particularism and relative autonomy. The extent of the provincial governors' hegemony over the Boyr Ahmad, for example, seldom exceeded the payment of a nominal and vaguely defined general tax collected by the khans, and some assurance against brigandage. In most cases, however, the tribal khans were coaxed into giving allegiance by the granting of honorific titles in recognition of their leadership. Since the two most important requisites of khanship are the interrelated elements of wealth and power, the affirmation of a khan's leadership from a prestigious source not only consolidated his political stance against contenders, it also brought wealth in the form of lavish gifts and a substantial portion of the taxes collected. The resultant equilibrium between the national government and the powerful tribes was, nevertheless, subject to the overall political climate and the permutations of the national power structure.

This state of affairs continued until the end of the Qajar dynasty. The early period of the intensely nationalistic Pahlavi dynasty (1925-) was characterized by a drastic change of attitude toward the tribal groups throughout the country. High among the priorities of Reza Shah was tribal pacification. After a series of bloody conflicts lasting from 1928 to 1933, major tribes--including the Boyr Ahmad--were brought under control. During the period between 1933 and Reza Shah's abdication in 1941, these tribes experienced unprecedented economic hardship and disorganization due to the policy of forced sedentarization. In 1941, taking advantage of the political vacuum and confusion following the Allied occupation of Iran, the imprisoned khans in Tehran made a dramatic escape and returned to their tribes. The annual migrations forbidden for over a decade were resumed with remarkable vitality.

After a relatively short period of laissez-faire, the national government adopted a less drastic but eminently more effective policy aimed primarily at destroying the corporate bases of tribal systems in Iran. The first step was to undermine the khans' power and authority by removing the economic support of their leadership, which depended to a great extent on the collection of tribal levies. The abolition of such levies was largely ignored, however, and tribesmen continued to support the khans voluntarily, though sometimes reluctantly. The most effective factor in the dissolution of the office of the khan, as well as all corporate interests in land, was the land reform law of 1962.

Although this long overdue, nationwide agrarian and rural reform was carried out with considerable effectiveness in other parts of the country, its implementation in tribal societies created difficulties, due largely to the fact that the planners either knowingly or unknowingly chose to ignore the patent differences between the tribal land-use and land-tenure systems and the absentee landlord-peasant systems characteristic of rural Iran.[9] The primary intent of the land reform, insofar as the tribes were concerned, was the parceling out of the khavanin's large estates among their tenants, retainers, personal servants, and members of their private armies--collectively referred to as malkhani or amaleh (lit., khan's property or menial worker).*

The effect of the removal of the paramount chiefs upon the tribal societies varied according to their political organization. The ramified, semi-anarchic system of the Boyr Ahmad, with its largely autonomous subtribes held together by a relatively diffuse political structure, absorbed the change with a minimum of hardship. Not too surprisingly, the majority of kadkhodas not only welcomed the power vacuum at the top, but also took an active part in deposing the khans by refusing them military assistance. A few even sided with the Army, and helped by organizing a militia to put down the last pockets of resistance. Such moves were not without precedence in the traditional power struggle between the khans and kadkhodas.

The few kadkhodas who supported the khans have lived to regret it, but those who shifted allegiance to the central government were left in office, some with regular subsidies and political favors, and assigned responsibility for the conduct of the tribesmen under their jurisdiction. These kadkhodas now serve as channels of communication and as broker-middlemen between the tribesmen and the military governor, who (ironically) employs the same manipulative tactics as the erstwhile khans in making sure that no kadkhoda becomes powerful enough to pose a threat to his authority. Similarly, extreme care is taken by the local administration to maintain the territorial integrity of each subtribe and never to allow the formation of coalitions or political blocs among them. For example, exogamous marriages among kadkhodas, which in the context of the traditional structure served as the first step toward political alliance, are now closely scrutinized by the local authorities.

The present administrative policy toward the Boyr Ahmad subtribes seems to be one of containment, rather than direct interference in their internal affairs or unnecessary curtailment

---

*Following the overthrow of Mohammed Mossadegh in 1953, certain tribes (including the Boyr Ahmad and Qashqai) became implicated in an abortive anti-government uprising, which accelerated the demise of the khavanin.

of the traditional functions of the leaders--as long as their actions are not contrary to the interests of the encapsulating structure. Given the palpable economic and political incentives and their chameleon tendencies, it is highly unlikely that the present kadkhodas would withdraw their allegiance from the central government in favor of an autochthonous political leader--much less a former khan. It is noteworthy that after the deposal of the khans, the abolition of khanships, and the crystallization of the subtribes, the Boyr Ahmad political system became fully compatible with that of the encapsulating structure.

To summarize the preceding discussion: effective transactions between the Boyr Ahmad and the national structure have up to now been limited largely to the political sphere. Insofar as the ecologic competition for natural resources and market integration are concerned, the effect of the encapsulating environment upon the Boyr Ahmad tribal system has been minimal.

Comparisons

To test the validity of our model, let us now examine the degree of encapsulation among two other pastoral tribes of Kuh Giluyeh--the Behmai[10] and the Taiyebi, using essentially the same three variables applied to the Boyr Ahmad (see p. 130 above). Ecologically, the part of the Zagros mountains inhabited by these tribes is even more rugged than the Boyr Ahmad country. Poor or nonexistent communications make it relatively inaccessible to the outside world. Travel to the regional market town--Behbahan--for the sale of occasional surpluses and for purchasing market goods is a major undertaking for the Behmai and Taiyebi tribesmen.

Because of the scanty agricultural yield, particularly among the Behmai, reliance on annual acorn-collecting is far greater than among even the poorest segment of the Boyr Ahmad. Seasonal migrations take place almost entirely within tribal territories, with a minimum of contact with other tribes. Transactions involving land or labor between these pastoral groups and any sedentary populations are very rare. For the great majority, the outside world is represented almost solely by the traveling trade partners and the ubiquitous "gendarmes."

Whereas during the last decade or so, the Boyr Ahmad have received a great deal of attention and some tangible benefits from the central government in the form of a few clinics (though hardly adequate for the entire population), animal vaccination, crop pesticides, formal education, and some communications--all under the national development program--the Behmai and Taiyebi have been generally neglected.

The contrast is reflected in the lament "Had we participated in or instigated an open revolt against the government, like the Boyr Ahmad, we too would have become the center of attention and not have been forgotten so completely. Is this any way to treat loyal subjects?"

The relative isolation of the Behmai and Taiyebi is further reflected in the austerity of their material culture, and in the simplicity of the people themselves. The Boyr Ahmad have many exaggerated accounts of their neighbors' "material and cultural poverty and backwardness," thinking themselves infinitely more sophisticated and civilized by comparison.

The political organization of these two tribes is deceptively similar to that of the Boyr Ahmad, with one significant difference: khans and kadkhodas belong to the same agnatic lineage, with a long tradition of internal rivalries, jealousies, and some serious conflicts. The office of the khan, however, is little more than ceremonial. For this reason khans are seldom assassinated or manipulated in and out of office, as among the Boyr Ahmad. Nevertheless, they play a vital role as mediators and in maintaining peace among the rival factions, though they enjoy little sanctioning power. Consequently, they are ineffective in mobilizing a significant portion of the population for concerted action. In addition, long-standing fear of their giant neighbor--the Boyr Ahmad--precludes any possibility of intertribal alliances. The khans, therefore, are very unlikely candidates to form coalitions or confederacies against the central authorities. Aware of these facts concerning the Behmai and Taiyebi, the government has felt little need to disturb the status quo and incur the financial burden of direct rule--as in the case of the Boyr Ahmad, for example. On the basis of the three aspects of encapsulation discussed above, these pastoral groups seem to represent an extreme position in which the effect of the national structure upon the tribal systems has so far been negligible--at best, minimal.

At the other end of the spectrum are the two major pastoral nomad tribes of Fars province in south Persia: the Qashqai and the Basseri. The overall ecologic conditions in Fars, southeast of the Boyr Ahmad, are drastically different from those further west in the Zagros mountains. Pasture resources are relatively poor and widely separated, sometimes by as much as several hundred kilometers. In contrast to the Kuh Giluyeh tribes, which seldom cross tribal boundaries in search of pasture, the Qashqai and Basseri in their migration routes between winter and summer quarters in Fars pass through vast expanses of nontribal regions dotted with villages and towns.

The process of coexistence between the nomads and sedentary populations exploiting the same ecologic niche is expressed in a variety of transactional modes. First, there is competition over the limited natural resources. A substantial improvement in medical services over the last two decades, translated into lower infant mortality and greater longevity, has led to an increase in the rate of population growth in Fars province.[11] On the other hand, the introduction of animal vaccination against endemic diseases has brought about a gradual rise in the nomads' animal population.

Second, with an increase in sedentary population, more and more pasture lands are being brought under cultivation. This process is exacerbated by a very thorough implementation of the 1962 land reform and land registration law in Fars province. The overall result which is beginning to emerge is an imbalance between human population, animal population, and pasture among the nomads. These processes have generated tension and conflict between the nomads and the sedentary populations, some of which involve long and costly litigation in towns and cities.

Third, as a coping device, the elite--particularly among the Qashqai--have been purchasing extensive tracts of land in winter and summer quarters and along the migration routes (as well as real estate in cities such as Shiraz and Isfahan). These lands are usually converted into orchards or rented to settled nomads under standard tenancy contracts. To get around the limitation imposed by the land reform law on the size of holdings by any one owner, these lands are registered under the names of different members of a chief's household. (Orchards are not affected by the law.)

With respect to literacy and higher education, these nomads--particularly the Qashqai--have been the targets of a very systematic and comprehensive program. For years the sons and daughters of wealthy tribesmen have been attending universities in Iran as well as abroad. Today an impressive number of Qashqai doctors, engineers, and educators are engaged in their professions in major cities as well as in their own tribes.

Innovative Qashqai and Basseri tribal entrepreneurs have been moving into the commercial sector previously monopolized by town merchants and traveling traders. These transactions imply a substantial degree of integration into the national market economy, in which the exchange of goods and services as well as land and labor play significant parts.

The political organization of the Qashqai and Basseri up to the middle of the 1950's was highly centralized in comparison to the Kuh Giluyeh tribes. As Barth has pointed out, the supreme chiefs, or Ilkhan, among the Basseri were

> traditionally granted a vast and not clearly delimited field of privilege and command, and power [was] conceived as

> emanating from him, rather than delegated to him by his subjects. . . . The scattered and constantly shifting tent camps of the Basseri [were] held together and welded into a unit by their centralized political system, culminating in the single office of the chief. . . . It [was] the fact of political unity under the Basseri chief which in the eyes of the tribesmen and outsiders alike constitute[d] them into a single tribe in the Persian sense.[12]

The Qashqai Ilkhans commanded no less power and privilege, though the political system was much more hierarchically organized than that of the Basseri. Supported by a sizable annual income derived from levies and investments, and a powerful private army, the Ilkhans coordinated migrations, allotted pastures, adjudicated disputes, and represented the tribe vis-à-vis the sedentary authorities. To safeguard the interests of the tribe they took an active part in national politics by sending deputies to the Majlis (national representative assembly) or by gaining important ministerial positions.

Most crucially, however, these tribes have in the past demonstrated the ability to form confederacies against a common enemy. Clearly, these features are in sharp contrast to the relatively diffuse, segmentary political system of the Boyr Ahmad and other tribes of Kuh Giluyeh. Interestingly, these are precisely the features which made the tribes incompatible with the political values and goals of the national government. The removal of the superstructure in these cases was not accompanied by a granting of greater autonomy to the subordinate chiefs of the subtribes, as among the Boyr Ahmad. Every subchief among the Qashqai, for example, has been assigned a military officer whose approval is necessary for most decisions. Thus, in these cases the overall picture is one of a greater degree of encapsulation by the larger society, implying some fundamental changes and far-reaching consequences for the encapsulated structures.

Conclusion

The principal aim of this paper has been to demonstrate, first, that the processes through which nomadic pastoral societies in Iran undergo structural change, largely as a result of external factors, do not seem to follow a uniform pattern; second, that such changes cannot be assumed ipso facto, or predicted simply because nomads have now become an integral part of a larger national political entity; third, that the degree of encapsulation experienced by pastoral nomads varies in proportion to the magnitude and intensity of transactions between them and the national structure.

The transactions involving various modes of exchange between the tribal societies and the larger encompassing structure are viewed essentially in terms of three important variables: (1) ecologic competition between nomads and sedentary populations over limited and diminishing natural resources, (2) the extent to which various tribal economies are integrated into the national market economy, and (3) the degree of compatibility between the tribal political structures and that of the encapsulating power--the national government. A comparison between the Boyr Ahmad and other pastoral nomads using these three variables has provided a test of the validity of the model. We have shown that the tribal systems can be conceptualized as falling along a continuum ranging from minimal encapsulation of such groups as the Behmai and Taiyebi to the partial encapsulation of the Boyr Ahmad and finally to the relatively complete encapsulation exemplified by the Qashqai and Basseri.

Footnotes

[1]F.G. Bailey, Strategems and Spoils: A Social Anthropology of Politics (Oxford: Blackwell, 1969), pp. 144-51.

[2]Ibid.

[3]Fredrik Barth, Nomads of South Persia: The Basseri Tribe of the Khamseh Confederacy (Oslo: University of Oslo Press, 1961). In this area, I find myself in some fundamental disagreement with Barth's position ("The Relationship Between Sedentarization and Social Stratification: A Critique of Barth" [paper delivered at the 71st Annual Meeting of the American Association of Anthropologists, Toronto, Canada, 1972]). Briefly, the data from various pastoral groups of southwest Iran, including the Boyr Ahmad, Qashqai, and those of the Kuh Giluyeh region, provide no evidence to support the idea that the "crucial factor" of sedentarization "generates" an economically homogeneous society with a highly centralized political organization, and that where sedentarization does not take place there is a stratified society (Barth, pp. 123-130).

[4]Fieldwork was carried out in Kuh Giluyeh, southwest Iran, during 1968-1970, supported by a National Institute of Mental Health Research Grant and Fellowship.

[5]These figures are not based on a reliable census, which is practically nonexistent for most tribal areas in Iran, but on an estimate arrived at by a research team of the Institute for Social Studies and Research of the University of Tehran.

The combined population of all nomads in Iran is variously estimated at 2-4 million--roughly 10-15 percent of the country's total inhabitants. Official sources, however, tend to give much lower figures than these.

[6]Haj Mirza Hassan Fassai, Tarikh-e-Fars Nameh Nasseri (Tehran: Senai Publishing Company, c. 1876). [In Persian.]

[7]Barth.

[8]Ibid.

[9]G. Fazel, "Social and Ecological Consequences of Land Reform among Pastoral Nomads in Iran" (paper delivered at the 32nd Annual Meeting of the Society for Applied Anthropology, Tucson, Arizona, 1973).

[10]Nader Afshar-Naderi, The Behmai Tribe (The Institute for Social Studies and Research, University of Tehran, Report No. 7, 1968). [In Persian.]

[11]Habibullah Payman, A Description and Analysis of the Economic, Social and Cultural Aspects of the Qashqai Tribe (The Institute of Health, University of Tehran, Publication No. 34, 1968). [In Persian.]

[12]Barth, p. 71.

THE SOCIAL IMPLICATIONS OF DEVELOPMENTAL POLICIES: A CASE STUDY FROM EGYPT

Abdalla Said Bujra

In 1959-1960 the Egyptian government introduced cooperative societies among the Bedouin of the Western Desert as part of its program to sedentarize them. At first--i.e., between 1959-1962--only 3 percent of the population joined the movement. By 1967, it was said that 62 percent of the population had become members of the cooperatives. In 1965 the government had established 39 cooperative societies, but the Bedouin themselves had set up 160 societies of their own. The result has been to strengthen lineage loyalties and traditional leadership, which is inconsistent with the basic principles of the cooperative movement.

The dramatic popularity of the cooperative movement and its effect on Bedouin society is the main concern of this paper. Why should Bedouin--most of whom had never heard of cooperative societies--suddenly be inflamed with enthusiasm for the cooperative movement? The official explanation by the government that its cooperative-socialist policy is successful because "it meets the needs of the people" is not satisfactory. The explanation of the Bedouin themselves that they are "natural socialists," and so respond quickly to socialist policies, is even more misleading. The situation is obviously more complex than either of these explanations.

My view is, first, that the cooperatives have had the effect of a catalyst on Bedouin society, in which surplus labor force has been released that has enabled the society to participate as an intermediary between two contrasting international economies. Second, the cooperative movement has provided a new area for lineage rivalry and has thus given new powers to the traditional leadership. The cooperative movement, then, even at this early stage of development, is already playing an important role in Bedouin social organization.

This paper is based on field research carried out in the Western Desert of Egypt between 1965-1967. The research was financed and carried out under the auspices of the Social Science Research Council of The American University in Cairo.

The Development of the Western Desert: 1959-1967

The population of the Western Desert is estimated at 115,000 people, with an animal population of about 600,000--mostly sheep. During World War II, a road and a railway line for transporting war supplies were built along the coast from Alexandria to the Libyan border. After the war this transport system brought no economic development of the region, the main reason being that the Western Desert was under military control, and movement of goods and people was strictly limited. Thus until 1959 the Western Desert was effectively cut off from the major political and economic changes taking place in the Delta. In 1959, it was estimated that over 70 percent of Bedouin income was from animal husbandry.

Immediately after the war, the Bedouin returned to their areas to find them full of mines, all buildings destroyed, and many wells blown up. They had no stock of barley to feed themselves, and most of them had lost considerable numbers of their animals, stored food, and capital equipment (such as tents and carpets). But they found a vast armory of destroyed vehicles, tanks, and arms and a considerable quantity of steel and cloth. The Bedouin collected tires, parts of vehicles, arms, clothes, and anything that merchants would buy, and smuggled them for sale in Alexandria. In return they bought food and cloth. These were in great demand in Libya at the time, and the Bedouin smuggled them across the border. This was facilitated by the fact that Bedouin on both sides of the Libya-Egypt border were allowed to move freely between the two countries in search of grazing. In this way, smuggling came to play an important part in Bedouin economy during the hard days after the war.

Since 1960, when the oil economy of Libya began to expand, a large number of Libyan Bedouin have drifted to towns.[1] The demand for both men and sheep increased sharply in Libya.[2] At the same time, the value of Libyan currency reached a high point at which one Libyan pound equalled two Egyptian pounds on the black market. These economic conditions attracted some Egyptian Bedouin to seek work in Libya. They also made the smuggling of sheep into Libya highly profitable. Thus, by the early 1960's the Bedouin found themselves occupying a crucial position between two contrasting economic situations. Libya, where Egyptian Bedouin were readily accepted as citizens, was prospering with an oil economy; its currency was valuable, and it imported European and Japanese luxury goods without restrictions. On the other hand, the large Egyptian market extending from Alexandria had an acute shortage of luxury goods because of import restrictions. The large Egyptian middle class in Alexandria was willing to pay astronomical prices for such European and Japanese goods as radios, cameras, cigarettes, clothes, shoes, perfumes, etc., which were available in Libya. Since there was a great demand for sheep from Egypt in Libya, the Bedouin, being in a position of contact with both economies, were clearly in a strategic position to act as intermediaries.

Between 1959 and 1962 two important developments took place in the Western Desert. First, in 1959 the Egyptian government set up a body called the General Desert Development Organization (GDDO). The aim of this organization is to reclaim new agricultural land in the Western Desert so that as many Bedouin as possible can settle as farmers. This sedentarization program, as it is called, is being carried out through cooperative societies, to which many Bedouin now belong. By 1965 about 14,000 Bedouin had become members of 39 cooperative societies. The GDDO, in its first five-year plan, spent approximately 12 million dollars in the Western Desert. Clearly these cooperative societies have come to play an important role in Bedouin economy.

The second development was the setting up in 1962 of a local system of government to replace the military rule that had previously existed. The Western Desert thus became like any other province of Egypt, with all the paraphernalia of bureaucracy attached to local governments. The Matrouh authorities, as they are now called, spent about $9 million in their first five-year plan to create the administration and extend the social services of free education, medical services, and social centers.

These two developments led to dramatic changes in the Western Desert in a short time. First, a huge sum of money was poured into the area within a very short period, giving its economy a tremendous boost. Second, an elaborate superstructure of bureaucracy--that of the Administration and the GDDO--was created overnight, with which the Bedouin had to deal. Nearly 8,000 government officials from the Nile Valley were brought into the Western Desert. Third, restrictions on the movement of goods and people between the Nile Valley and the Western Desert were lifted, and there was a great expansion of rail, road, and air transport. This immediately incorporated the Western Desert into the wider economy of the Nile Valley and, at the same time, brought a flood of Nile Valley people into the town of Mersa Matrouh. Fourth, the government encouraged tourism to Mersa Matrouh, turning it into what the newspapers call "the Egyptian Riviera." By 1966 the town of Mersa Matrouh had a resident population of 12,000 and a tourist population of 50,000 during the three summer months of June to August.[3] It had also become the best-known market for smuggled goods in the country.

How have these forces of change introduced within such a short period affected the Bedouin? In my opinion, the cooperative societies are playing a very significant role as agents of change, since they affect the majority of Bedouin and touch on an important and sensitive point in their traditional politico-economic system.[4] I will therefore concentrate my analysis on the reactions of the Bedouin to the cooperatives. However, let me first briefly describe Bedouin economy.

Traditional Bedouin Economy

The Western Desert is a very dry country with an annual rainfall of between 2 to 4 inches. Bedouin expect two good years, two disastrous years, and three intermediate years in every seven-year cycle. When rain falls, it is spread unevenly--coming down heavily in some areas and lightly in others. The region has three types of land. Along the coastal belt (about ten miles deep), winter cultivation is commonly practiced, and there are some pockets of good farming land. Bedouin in this area practice both cultivation and animal husbandry. Almost all the "free born" tribes live in this area; these tribes have a status superior to the category of tribes known as the "attached" or "tied" tribes. This second category of tribes lives beyond the coastal belt, up to about twenty miles inland. In this inland area, the land is rather stony and cultivation is not possible. During the winter, however, shrubs and water points are available there for grazing, while the coastal belt has no grazing at this time because most of the land is under cultivation. Thus most of the animals from the coastal belt are moved inland for grazing during the winter. The inland tribes are dependent almost entirely on animal husbandry, and members of these tribes are often hired as shepherds. Further south of this inland area, the land is dry, barren, and inhospitable. No one lives there.

Bedouin live in camp units or settlements varying in size from 20-50 people. Those on the coastal belt are now rapidly building houses, turning former camp units into settlements. Those inland still live in tents, and the traditional camp unit is the same. Both camps and settlements are made up of close agnates divided into extended and nuclear families, the former being the most common type. The units have common ownership of grazing land and wells. Cultivated land is also sometimes commonly owned, but in the majority of cases such land has been divided among the members of the unit.

Bedouin insist that their economy centers on animal husbandry, that their stock is their main form of capital, and that wealth is measured in terms of animals. Animal husbandry entails supplying enough food and water for the animals throughout the year. The main problem is the winter period between October and April. At this time of year all edible grass and shrubs generally disappear from the ground along the coast. Between October and December the problem becomes especially serious because many of the female animals are pregnant and require good food. In times of drought many animals die during this period. The usual practice is to send the animals inland for grazing and to supplement their food supply with hay which is stored from cultivation or bought. In times of drought, people move to the edges of the Nile Delta for grazing.

Bedouin consider that a family needs an animal stock of about 60 sheep and goats as a minimum for survival without doing supplementary work such as cultivation or working as a shepherd.[5] When a family's livelihood depends entirely on its animal stock, its economic activity follows the normal pattern of animal husbandry in the area. Feeding the animals entails being inland for grazing during the winter and on the coast during the summer. Milking, making butter, culling, shearing, marketing of offspring, and generally looking after the animals--all these are essential activities in a herding economy. The Bedouin tribes inland also need barley and hay--both of which are essential food for themselves and their animals. These are acquired in many ways. Bedouin with surplus animal stock may trade them to buy barley and hay, or they may acquire land for their cultivation. Many work in harvesting during the summer or as shepherds during the winter. The need for barley and hay forces the majority of the inland tribes to divert part of their labor force to fulfill this need.

Among the Bedouin on the coastal belt, however, animal husbandry is supplemented with cultivation by many people. Barley is grown between September and December. Cultivation entails tilling and ploughing the land, planting and guarding the barley, and harvesting and storing it during the summer. But the Bedouin who cultivate are forced to divert part of their labor force to feed and look after their animals.

Bedouin living in the two areas thus emphasize different aspects of the same economic cycle. In a coastal settlement with 12 adult working men, 75 percent of the men said they were engaged in cultivation and only 8 percent in animal husbandry (i.e., as shepherds). On the other hand, two inland camp units had 7.5 and 20 percent respectively of their adult males as cultivators, with 70 and 60 percent respectively engaged entirely in animal husbandry.

This economic interdependence is an ideal basis for large-scale economic cooperation between the tribes of the two areas. If one can speculate, this may in fact have been the case in the past, since the inland tribes were inferior and tied politically and (presumably) economically to those on the coast. This traditional relationship has been breaking down for some time now, however.

The economic process described poses a serious dilemma to the coastal tribes, who are the majority of the Bedouin. This dilemma, which all Bedouin face, stems from the fact that during the winter period (between September and March) a Bedouin family faces two crucial economic situations. On the one hand, this is the period for tilling and ploughing the land, planting and guarding barley. Thus a concentration of its labor force on cultivation is important at this time. On the other hand, this is also the period when animals need to be taken inland for grazing. During this period, then, most Bedouin families split up--some going inland with the animals while others remain with the cultivation.[6] Some wealthy families solve this problem by hiring shepherds. Others cooperate with agnates, whereby an entire family moves inland leaving its cultivation to relatives. The same problem faces the inland tribes. During the winter they must remain inland for grazing. But this is also the period in which those who cultivate must be in the coastal area. This economic necessity to split a family's labor force has probably been an important factor inhibiting the accumulation of capital--in terms of cultivating more land and increasing the number of animals.

A second important factor in Bedouin economic organization is the necessity for Bedouin to live in camp units or settlements. Membership in these agnatic camp units is essential for acquiring rights to use the commonly owned grazing land and wells, and to own cultivated land. But membership in these units entails considerable economic cooperation between the members--e.g., the maintenance of camp wells, the use of search parties for lost sheep, the sharing of hospitality to visitors, reciprocity in the daily domestic field, and the ultimate security of finding help in case of a major economic disaster. Bedouin families are thus involved in a network of economic ties within the camp unit. These ties are reinforced by kinship and political ties within the agnatic camp unit. A family cannot survive as an independent economic unit outside the camp's economic network. To foster economic individualism, as the sedentarization program aims to do, means breaking down this economic interdependence within a camp. Obviously this will be a major obstacle facing the program.

As noted earlier, in 1959 the Egyptian government introduced the cooperative movement into the Western Desert. The aim was to increase cultivated land in the area by providing agricultural services, economic cooperation, and the improvement of water resources. A few societies were set up in pockets along the coast where good farming land was found. In 1963, however, the Egyptian government, with the help of the UN-FAO program, offered to provide food and fodder to all those Bedouin who would join the cooperative societies. Membership in a society was restricted to those who were engaged in cultivation and who would take immediate steps to plant trees on their land. The idea was that by providing food and fodder to Bedouin during the three bad winter months, many of them would be encouraged to take up cultivation and settle on the land. Since 1963, membership in cooperative societies has risen steeply and dramatically. For example, in one society set up in 1962 with a membership of 30 people, the membership jumped to 87 in 1963, to 530 in 1964, and to 566 in 1965. What are the effects of the cooperative movement on Bedouin society?

The services provided by the cooperative societies affect the most important aspects of Bedouin economy. To start with, both the food and fodder supplied to members of the cooperative society are a form of supplementary income. The fodder given to the Bedouin during the three months of the winter go a long way to help the Bedouin feed his animal herd without sending them inland for grazing. This is important for two reasons. First, it relieves Bedouin manpower from going inland at just the time when it is needed for cultivation. Second, fodder is a healthier food than the poor shrubs that the animals get from grazing. The effect of good food during the three months (October to December) when the female animals are pregnant, along with the widespread veterinary service introduced with the cooperatives, has on the whole increased the animal stock of the Bedouin. With animal stock being the major form of Bedouin capital, one would expect wide repercussions on the total economy.

Another widely used service of the cooperatives is the supplying of tractors. Tractors enable Bedouin to cultivate large areas without the use of all the male members of a family, as was previously the case. One result is that more land is cultivated and more barley harvested. More important, however, is the fact that some male members of the family are now relieved from the arduous work of ploughing and tilling the land. Some of these men, relieved from agricultural work and from herding, are free to participate in other economic activities outside the cultivation-herding cycle. The extra income earned by these men is used in two ways. First, it is used to employ outsiders who come seasonally for harvesting, so that the Bedouin can continue in their new occupations. Second, it is used for trade in animals to increase the family's stock.

The effect of the cooperative movement has basically been twofold. It has increased the animal stock of the Bedouin, and it has released part of the Bedouin labor force to take part in a wider economy. What are the implications of these two effects?

The extent of increase in the animal stock is difficult to estimate, since figures are hard to obtain. But after taking a census in 1963 and another in 1965, the authorities were greatly alarmed at the problem of over-grazing from increased stock. To deal with this problem, they plan to introduce a scheme to reduce the size of the herds in the area. For our purposes, however, it is the effect of the increase in the animal stock which is important. One effect is the revival of animal markets in the whole region. However, instead of prices falling as a result of the increase in the supply of animals, there has been a great inflation in prices and an ever-increasing demand. The main reason for this is that sheep are bought to be smuggled to Libya, where prices are high. In 1966 the government estimated that between 50 and 70 percent of the 250,000 annual marketable animal stock were being illegally exported into Libya by the Bedouin. The markets along the road to Libya are a good indication of this trade. The nearer the market is to the Libyan border, the higher are the prices of animals in the market. The large-scale smuggling of animals into Libya has had two effects:

1. Many people have become involved in the trading cycle with Libya. It is carried out by big and small traders as well as by those who actually transport the animals into Libya.

2. The high prices which animals fetch in the market as well as the large profits derived from sales in Libya have on the whole appreciably increased the income of the Bedouin.

Markets and villages have recently sprung up along the road to Libya, and they have become important trading centers with many little shops and cafes run by Bedouin. These are places where Bedouin can buy all their food requirements and obtain other services. The expenditure pattern of the Bedouin has changed as their income has increased. The town of Mersa Matrouh has become an important center with a population of 7,000 Bedouin engaged in all kinds of economic activities. The major part of the surplus labor released from Bedouin camp units has been absorbed into the activities of smuggling and trading.

The large-scale animal trade with Libya is counterbalanced by an opposite movement of goods from Libya to the Nile Delta on an even larger scale. As pointed out earlier, Libya imports large quantities of luxury goods from all over the world. Items like transistor radios, tape recorders, and cameras from Japan, as well as clothes, cigarettes, shoes, and many small portable goods from Europe and America, are available in Libya at cheap prices. These are items which are in great demand in the Delta, where they fetch very high prices. Thus a large illegal trade from Libya to Alexandria in these goods is carried out by the Bedouin.

This trade is important in that it involves a large number of people and large sums of money. The authorities estimate that nearly 60 percent of the Bedouin are involved in one way or another in smuggling. The little shops and cafes serve as important points for hiding and transmitting goods. In the town of Mersa Matrouh there is a large and well-attended daily market where smuggled goods pass hands. This market is held at 4 P.M. At 5 P.M. a train leaves the town for Alexandria, and the police raid this train at least three times a week.[7] Many of the 50,000 summer tourists go to Mersa Matrouh partly to buy smuggled goods. Being gullible customers they are an important factor in this trade. Apart from individual transactions, there are merchants who carry on smuggling on a large scale, using trucks, large numbers of trained donkeys, and trains. Such people are found mainly in the border village of Salloum and in the town of Mersa Matrouh. This kind of smuggling is now an important part of the Bedouin economy.

I have shown that the introduction of cooperative societies among the Bedouin has resulted in an increase in their animal stock and in the release of labor from the traditional economy. This (I have argued) has enabled the Bedouin to participate more effectively in a wider economic system in which they play the role of intermediary between Libya and the Nile Valley. They are able to play this economic role because of their strategic position between the two contrasting economies and because of the removal of restrictions in the area. The cooperatives have obviously acted as catalysts in this process of economic change, and the Bedouin recognize this.

The movement of labor from camp units and settlements to new occupations can be seen from the following table:

PERCENTAGES IN OCCUPATIONS

	Adult Men (N)	Farming Only	Farming and Herding	Animal Husbandry and Animal Trade	Non-Traditional Occupations	Total Percent
Lineage Dispersed in Separate Districts in Coastal Area	38	10%	56%	--	34%	100%
Segment of Lineage Settlement in Coastal Area	12	--	75	8%	17	100
Camp Unit: Inland	13	--	7.5	69.5	23	100
Camp Unit: Inland	5	--	20	60	20	100

Another significant effect of the cooperative movement has been to sharpen the traditional wealth differences between the inland tribes and those on the coastal belt--i.e., between the free and the tied tribes. The cooperative societies are all in the coastal area, since their primary aim is to make people settle as farmers. Membership in a cooperative society requires ownership of cultivated land. This not only gives advantages to the coastal tribes who own cultivable land, but cuts off a large number of the inland tribes from the cooperative movement. Yet it is these inland tribes who most need the help of fodder for their animals. Thus while coastal tribes are now able to increase their cultivation and animal stock and also participate in a wider economy, the inland tribes are on the whole outside this process. The result is a tendency toward greater disparity in wealth between the two categories of tribes.

The inland tribes, though denied the advantages of the cooperative movement, have nevertheless been able to take advantage of some of the new opportunities. The great demand for sheep and goats and the high prices obtained in the markets have attracted many animal traders from these tribes. More important, their strategic position inland and far away from police detection has involved them in the smuggling and transportation of sheep into Libya. On the other hand, the coastal tribes, living as they do along the tarmac road and the rail line next to it, are best suited to smuggle goods in the opposite direction--from Libya to Alexandria. This they do by manipulating the transportation system and the extensive network of little shops and cafes manned by relatives. Thus inland tribes tend to smuggle sheep into Libya while coastal tribes smuggle goods to the Delta.

The Bedouin recognize the important role played in the Bedouin economy by the cooperative societies, as is shown by the steep rise in their membership. The 39 societies now in existence have been set up along the coast beside the main road. Each society covers a specific area, and to people living in the area, control of the society is obviously important. Ideally this is achieved by having one society cover the territory of one lineage, thus avoiding interlineage competition. This is not possible in the Western Desert, however, because of the settlement pattern of the tribes. Although these tribes have a classic segmentary political organization, there are no neat inclusive territories of tribes in which all their segments live. Any given tribe or clan in the Western Desert is scattered all over the region. There is no lineage which is not dispersed. Thus a cooperative society in any area will have a mixed membership drawn from many lineages of different tribes. Lineage competition for the control of a cooperative society generally follows its introduction. But why is control of a society so important?

Membership in a cooperative society is the first step toward receiving help from the society. Help in food and fodder depends on the economic status of the member, and this is judged by the Council of the society. The quantity of food and fodder a person gets depends on the size of his family and his stock of animals. It is the President of the cooperative society who ultimately decides on the reliability of a person's statement as to the size of his family and herds. The President thus occupies a powerful position. A lineage clearly has a better chance of getting preferential treatment if its representatives control the Council, and especially the office of President. Those elected to the Council must in turn look after their supporters. The ideal situation is for a lineage to have its own cooperative society. Given the settlement pattern described above, this would clearly lead to a proliferation of societies all over the region--and this is in fact what happened.

When the cooperative societies were first introduced, only a few people joined. But as soon as it was realized that membership had many advantages, many people flocked to join. Within a year, many cooperative societies were set up all over the area. For instance, in the village of Barrani, a cooperative society was set up with 584 members. Within a year, twenty other cooperative societies had sprung up in the area covered by the Barrani cooperative. Of its 584 members, 411 withdrew to join the new societies on the basis of lineage affiliation. The original cooperative was left with 173 members, mostly from one lineage. The twenty new societies were set up by leaders of lineages who became Presidents of their respective societies and used their houses as offices. In the district of Barrani as a whole, the GDDO established four cooperative societies. By 1965 there were 43 cooperative societies in the district. On the average each society had only 64 men. In the same year, the GDDO had established in the whole Western Desert only 39 cooperative societies. But the Bedouin by themselves had established an estimated 160 societies, with an average of 70 members each. The Bedouin set up their own societies in order to maintain control and derive the maximum benefit from the services they provide. In this way smaller lineages avoided the disadvantages of being swamped by larger lineages.

When the government realized that the Bedouin were not conforming to the ideals of the cooperative movement, it amalgamated by law all the 160 Bedouin societies into the 39 official societies established by the GDDO. This created fierce competition within the cooperative societies. Sometimes lineage segments withdrew from one society in order to join a distant society where a segment of their own lineage had control. But the possibility of shifts of this kind is limited. On the whole the pattern of mixed memberships remained. In this situation the mathematics of voting is extremely important, as a few examples will show:

Example 1. A society was set up in 1961 with 21 members. Their numerical strength was as follows:

	In the Society	In the Council
Lineage A	7 members	2: President and Secretary
Lineage B	4 members	2: Treasurer and Member
Lineage C	4 members	1: Member
Six lineages, each with one member	6 members	5: Members
Total	21 members	10

Election to the Council was carried out on the basis of these 21 members. Since then no election has taken place. By 1965 this society had a membership of 638.

Example 2. A society was set up in 1962 with a membership of 96. By 1965 it had a membership of 310 persons. These were divided among lineages as follows:

	In the Society	In the Council
Lineage A	80 members	2: President and Member
Lineage B	50 members	2: Treasurer and Member
Lineage C	40 members	1: Secretary
Four lineages, each with an average of 15 men	140 members	5: Members
Total	310 members	10

The Council which was elected in 1962 is still in power.

Lineage loyalties dominate elections and decide the composition of the Councils. Most of the societies have so far had only one election. These elections were held at the time of the establishment of the society. All members who had joined the society at that time were eligible to vote. But even with a small membership, the strength of the lineages was a decisive factor in the control of the Council. Since then, the increase in membership and the amalgamation of the many societies into the few that are now officially recognized has meant that the numerical strengths of the lineages have changed and the mathematics of voting have become more complex. The next series of elections will obviously show this. But at present most of those who came into power are still in control of the 39 cooperative societies.

Who are these people? The pattern whereby one of the 39 cooperative societies was established was as follows: Officials of the GDDO would approach a leader of a dominant lineage of an area and ask him to help them form a society. Such a man would then get people from his own lineage and a few from other lineages to join the society by buying shares. Whatever number of people the man rallied to join the cooperative, the GDDO officials would then form a Council of 5 members, and generally make the lineage leader the President. Other members of the Council would be elected, but they also would tend to be leaders of their lineages. Thus traditional lineage leaders were able to get into positions of authority in the new institutions of the cooperative movement, and their powers have since been strengthened by the growing importance of the cooperative societies in Bedouin life.

The Bedouin, then, have responded to the cooperative movement in terms of group loyalties. This is indicated by lineage competition for control of the societies and by the election of traditional leaders to positions of authority in the cooperatives. These leaders have on the whole used their new powers to the advantage of their kinsmen who elected them. Whenever possible they have manipulated the rules of the cooperatives in order to give more fodder and food to their supporters, and to give them priority in the use of tractors at the crucial time of rainfall when everyone wants the tractors. But some of these leaders have used their powers for their own self-interest and against the interests of their supporters. Many have been accused by the people of giving them less fodder than they are entitled to, and selling the rest on the black market and pocketing the money. To what extent then can one say that there is a growing trend in which self-interest--i.e., individualism--is a dominant principle in Bedouin behavior, overriding the traditional principles of lineage loyalties?

The government's program ignores Bedouin loyalties to their groups at different levels. It has acted positively against these groups--first by creating new single interest groups in the form of cooperative societies, and second by amalgamating those societies formed by the Bedouin on the basis of lineage membership. The ideal of the government is to see Bedouin families settled on their farms and living as independent economic units, but acting corporately in specified economic activities as members of cooperative societies. This ideal is not possible to realize at this stage of development for a number of reasons. First, the cooperatives have not been developed to the stage of acting as economic units in production or marketing. At present their main function is as points of distribution for aid and agricultural services. Second, because of their present role (as I have argued earlier), the cooperatives have provided a new area for lineage rivalry, thus reinforcing traditional loyalties. Third, Bedouin families still depend to a large extent on economic cooperation within the settlement for their survival. This is to say that although Bedouin gain economic advantages from the cooperatives, and that--like all people--they act for their self-interest within a given area of choice, nevertheless the majority cannot afford to act against the interests of the group. But in return for the economic security the settlement provides for its member , they have to conform to certain rules. For instance, a Bedouin cannot sell the land he owns to anyone outside the settlement group, even though the government will allow the sale, for this is against the rules of the group. Thus most Bedouin will not act against the interests of the group even if their action would be economically advantageous. Very few of the Bedouin living in town who are economically independent of their settlement have taken the institutionally permitted step of opting out of the group. This is because a Bedouin living in town is still involved in a web of kinship and political ties with his group. For those living in the settlements, economic cooperation is essential. Economic individualism, then, is measured in terms of breaking ties with the group. Those few leaders who have acted against the interests of their groups can be described as "temporary individualists." Sanctions against them will probably be imposed in the next election.

In sum, the introduction of the cooperative movement in Bedouin society has resulted in unexpected and unintended consequences. First, the cooperatives have enabled the Bedouin to make use of their strategic position in order to participate in an extensive smuggling trade. Second, the traditional wealth differentiation between the "noble" and the "inferior" tribes is, in a sense, now being officially increased. Third, the cooperative movement, far from breaking down lineage loyalties, has strengthened them and with them the traditional leadership.

Between 1967 and 1970, the cooperative movement was expected to enter a new stage in its development. During this stage, the societies were to take over the marketing of Bedouin animals, wool, and barley. They were to be given power to reduce the animal stock of individuals by withholding aid. Clearly the movement would be entering a crucial stage. Since I have no information on what has happened since 1967, I could only speculate concerning the continued effect of the cooperative movement on Bedouin; speculation, however, is the antithesis of scientific inquiry.

Footnotes

[1]Libyan population distribution in 1962 was as follows: 35 percent urban, 40 percent rural, and 25 percent nomadic (Middle East and North Africa Yearbook, 1962).

[2]The per capita gross national product in Libya in 1951 was estimated at $40. This figure began to rise very sharply after 1960, with oil production. By 1967 it was $1000, and the estimate for 1973 is $1700 (New York Times, February 9, 1969).

[3]In 1959 the estimated annual number of tourists to Mersa Matrouh was 2000 (Al-Ahram, December 7, 1959).

[4]My analysis of the role of the cooperative societies in the Western Desert applies to the period between 1965 and 1967. In 1967 plans were in hand to expand the activities of the cooperative societies. How far these have been carried out I do not know.

[5]Counting 5 persons per family, an estimated population of 115,000 persons will give 23,000 families. The estimated 600,000 sheep and goats in the Western Desert divided between 23,000 families gives about 25 sheep and goats per family.

[6]"After the first showers of November, barley is sown and the young men soon move with their flock to the pastures [inland] leaving the older people to look after the fields. As the dry season advances, the flock are moved northwards [to the coast] to cultivated lands so as to be nearer to fodder or water holes" (A.M. Abou-Zeid, "The Sedentarization of Nomads in the Western Desert of Egypt," International Social Science Journal, Vol. XI, No. 4 (1959), p. 553.

[7]The extent of smuggling, the methods used, and the steps taken by the government were described in many lengthy newspaper articles during 1967, especially in Al-Ahram, Al-Akhbar, and Akher Saa.

LEADERSHIP AND TRANSITION IN BEDOUIN SOCIETY: A CASE STUDY

G.J. Obermeyer

Introduction

This paper deals with political change in a Bedouin society by focusing on one mechanism of transition deemed particularly important to the anthropologist. It bears on the role of a type of tribal leader--the "cultural broker"--in the transformation of his society. The backdrop of the study is a world in which traditional symbols and meanings have disappeared or are decaying, and where the structural principles of the old system have lost their validity. In their wake there is a new consciousness emerging, an awareness of a better life to come. In examining this phenomenon I have taken my cue from Weber's conception of political action as that "which seeks to encompass both the very great limitations that every social situation imposes upon the individual and the great opportunities for action that are inherent in the instability of social structures."[1] The specific political problem of concern here pertains to the role of key individuals in society.

For the purposes of this paper, "politics" does not refer primarily to Weber's idea of "conflict" and "struggle" between groups[2] or to Easton's notion of the authoritative allocation of scarce values in society.[3] Both are useful concepts, but where transition and its vicissitudes are our main concern, we should perhaps be guided by a more apposite definition. Ernest Gellner discussing the transition says:

> Politics is the rule by the Wise--i.e. those who have access to the tribal magic of industrial society and can initiate their own tribes into it; and politics is also the emergence of the Real and the Rational from the merely manifest and not-so-good; in concrete terms, industrial men are struggling to emerge from non-industrial ones.[4]

All human groups are characterized by leaders. Lévi-Strauss claims there are leader-types or chiefs "because there

---

The field work on which this paper is based was made possible by the Social Research Center of The American University in Cairo.

are . . . men who . . . enjoy prestige for its own sake, feel a strong appeal to responsibility, and to whom the burden of public affairs brings its own reward."[5] He cautions anthropologists to pay more attention to the idea of "natural leaders" when developing the study of political institutions.

One type of "natural leader" has been defined by Eric Wolf as the "broker"--a "nation-oriented person" whose basic function is to relate "community-oriented persons" (who have the desire but not the means to improve their life chances) to the wider political system of the nation-state.[6] The "broker" is one who seeks power outside his local community and can "operate both in terms of community-oriented and nation-oriented expectations." Wolf also notes that brokerage carries its own rewards.[7] Clifford Geertz has further developed the concept of "broker" by highlighting the creative as well as the manipulative aspect of the role. The "cultural broker" is an instance of "vigorous, imaginative leadership, able to play a cultural middleman role between peasant and metropolitan life, and so create an effective juncture between traditional cultural patterns and modern ones."[8]

The "cultural broker," then, is not just a creative individual in a traditional society. The concept has no meaning outside the context of the transition. The "broker" is a cultural role and phenomenon which goes beyond Goldenweiser's "primitive individual" who is caught in an involuted maze wherein "change can only be an elaboration, leading, as an ultimate limit, to seemingly insane complexity."[9]

Structural Background of Bedouin Society

The territory of the 'Aishaibāt tribe, a sub-unit of the 'Ali Aḥmar tribe of the Awlād 'Ali, is located in the northwestern coastal zone on the northern edge of the Egyptian Western Desert. The 'Aishaibāt population of about 3,000 persons (approximately 1,300 males and 1,700 females) lives on the coastal plain and in the cultivable _wadis_ about 16 kilometers west of the provincial capital of Marsa Maṭrūḥ. The inhabited area measures about 6 kilometers east to west along the coast by 15 kilometers north to south--extending into the desert as far as the Libyan Plateau. The area is made up of three ecological zones: the coastal orchard and garden area, where olives and mint are the chief cash crops; the barley and sheep-goat pasture area south and back from the coast; and the southern pastoral area of camel grazing.

The economic base of society in this area is undergoing transformation. Increasing concern for olive-growing by the government and the Bedouin and a growing respect for modern agricultural and hydraulic methods by the Bedouin, along with a relatively successful governmental community development program, are effectively turning pastoral tribesmen into sedentary farmers and gardeners.

'Aishaibāt Bedouin society is characterized by certain structural principles, the most pervasive being the rule of patrilineality. According to this principle, a person born into a sub-lineage unit (or "tertiary segment" in Peters' classification)[10] gains jural status in the wider political system which embraces the whole Awlād 'Ali tribe. In theory, the unilinear principle and its corollary--the corporate group--are the effective bases for dividing Bedouin society into social and political groupings.

In the Bedouin politics of this part of the Western Desert, the tertiary sub-lineage segment (bait) and the secondary lineage segment ('āila) are the functionally significant units. But only the bait is a true corporate group, in the sense that it alone has a discernible authority structure and possesses autonomy. Each lineage segment, from the tribe (qabīla) to the smallest segment (bait), claims its own territory (mintaqa). Although common kinship and property relations with reference to an authority structure usually define political groups, other patterns of Bedouin behavior lead to associative relationships which may or may not affect the ideologically dominant lineage principle. Such patterns relate to residence, cognatic ties, and the formation of contractual ties.

Thus, in the classical sense, the principle of government of the 'Aishaibāt is the complementary opposition of groups which are characterized by institutional uniformities of structure, ideology, and procedure.[11] This articulation is either clarified or confused by other links, the most important of which is contract. The idea of contract is stressed here because it is the verifying principle of corporation at the bait level, and the logic and prerequisite for corporateness at the secondary segmentary level. As a principle of association, it may at times override all other structural principles.

The corporate group is "entirely a matter of the presence of a person in authority, with or without an administration staff,"[12] referred to as a "corporation sole" or "public officer," a role first defined by Sir Henry Maine.[13] In 'Aishaibāt society, such a corporate office exists at the bait level of Bedouin political structure. It is an elective post, having only one incumbent at a time. This office is the constitutive symbol of the group; it makes morality and political sentiments meaningful, sanctions legitimate, and solidarity possible.

In Bedouin society, the solidarity of the corporate group has been explained by Robertson Smith in terms of a covenant of blood responsibility: a compact of mutual accountability in which the group has rights in rem over its members.[14] In the Western Desert, the concept which derives from this pre-Islamic basis of contract is that of the 'āqila. The 'āqila (pl. 'awāqil) is the term applied to both the public office and the group itself--e.g., 'āqilit fulan. Members of this group claim a share in the indemnity--i.e., the blood money (dīya)--and each member must contribute equal shares to the dīya when it comes due on the group. Furthermore, each corporate member of the 'āqila, or bait, is bound to swear the oath (yamīn) in support of a lineage-mate accused of a crime or falsehood in matters of litigation. The 'āqila is a contractual relationship par excellence.

Through the years, the contracts of the 'awāqil have become formalized and set in well-defined terms, though they vary in content from lineage to lineage. Such a code becomes the basis of entering into relations with other groups. Usually, but not always, groups related through contract are also related through an immediate ancestor. Duplicate copies of what is called ittifāq al-'awāqil ("the agreement of the wise men") are drawn up and ratified by the respective leaders of the tertiary groups involved. Just as in the corporate group per se, all members adhering to the wider bond swear to uphold their contractual partners in matters of blood-revenge, compensation for blood, and swearing the oath. Another right for which the individual can expect support from group members at the wider lineage level is the one he has over his father's brother's daughter (bint 'amm). Although bint 'amm marriage is only a preferred practice in Bedouin society, the right of a man to decide whom, when, and if his cousin will marry is strongly prescribed. A girl may refuse the son of her uncle (ibn 'amm), but she and her family risk the possibility of violent confrontation and the certainty of political censure should she try to marry someone without the permission of her cousin.

The basic values which underwrite such contracted political relations take their meaning from the wider system of legal norms which binds all of the Bedouin of the Western Desert and Cyrenaica together into one loosely connected political system. This wider normative system is expressed in the customary legal process of Bedouin law known as the 'awaiyid Awlād 'Ali ("the customs of Awlād 'Ali").

The corporate authority structure in relation to wider corporate categories and a customary legal system is the key to understanding and explaining Bedouin society. But the contractual ties are themselves political arrangements, and thus power groups emerge to complicate this structural simplicity. Such power relations along with the social relations based on cognatic bonds give rise to a dynamic political field where at times even the solidarity and effectiveness of local agnatic groups are undermined. It is in this relatively unstructured field of power relations that the individual is given most latitude to exercise his creative resourcefulness and ingenuity.

The Cultural Broker

In 'Aishaibāt Bedouin society we have seen that the role of the 'āqila is legitimate, public, and representative, and that it is distributed and functions with reference to corporate groups. In addition, there are power roles which have no legitimate or representative function in the segmentary system, and give rise to structures and modes which combine and can be "quite unlike the articulations in the lineage system."[15] These structures and modes of power represent the dynamic bases of real leadership and transition in Bedouin society.

One such structure in Bedouin society is a quasi-group defined by high status. The economic and political advantages of the members of this group set them apart from others. Such a group corresponds to Weber's notion of a Stand, or "status group," whose members are not organized into an association but are differentiated from the rest of society by the amount of "status honor" which they possess.[16] Their prestige derives from traditional sources of wealth and gives them access to the social and market situations of the administrative town of Marsa Matrūḥ. They benefit from associational ties with members of the central government while maintaining communal ties in the desert. Accruing "status honor" in one system augments it in the other. Most members of this group are nation-oriented and extol the economic benefits of the new way of life over against the old.

Members of the "status group" come from the wealthiest and most influential ineages in the desert. Wealth in 'Aishaibāt society is measured in terms of sheep, land, and olives. In a comparison of wealth, members of the "status group" owned on the average of 661 olive trees, compared to an average of 86 for all others in the society; 402 head of sheep compared to 30; and 91 acres of land compared to 5.

Though wealth is a major determinant of status in Bedouin society, the most important way to accrue "status honor" is through playing the role of mediator in conflict situations. The intervention of a third party is an effective way to forestall formal litigation at the level of the office of 'āqilā. The third party who intervenes in quarrels is designated by the Bedouin as the rajal khair ("good man"). The function of the rajal khair is structured only to the degree that parties seeking his intervention agree to abide by his final decision. In comparison to the role of the 'āqila, the role of the rajal khair has no well-defined set of rights and obligations attached to it.

The power of the 'āqila is limited by the very structure of the role. The role of the rajal khair, being less institutionalized and structured, is less confined with respect to the kind and amount of influence the role-player might exert.[17] Such a role can be highly flexible in the field of power relations.

The rajal khair operates across group and lineage lines to widen his support structure. He is able to do this because, as the Bedouin say, a man depends on the rajal khair, knowing that the litigant will "save his rights"--i.e., will salvage his honor. Litigation is entered into with the understanding that neither party will emerge a "loser." On the other hand, the 'āqila is expected to be dispassionate and objective. He must rule solely on the basis of the rightness or wrongness of acts. As one informant said:

> Both are one [i.e., the 'āqila and the rajal khair], for both the 'āqila and the rajal khair can end a problem. The rajal khair tries to solve the problem, but only the 'āqila judges (yaḥkum). The rajal khair worries about the feelings of the two men involved, but the 'āqila cares only about justice and what is right. . . . The rajal khair does not want the two men to lose one another. It is a friendly way to solve problems.

As a member of the "status group," the rajal khair also provides aid in times of financial need. In some ways, the wealth of the rajal khair is the wealth of the community. But as Peters notes concerning the Cyrenaican case,[18] generosity--not being entirely altruistic--wins repute, and repute is an important aspect of political power. The rajal khair then, as a member of the "status group" and a "broker," can afford to spend time and money in courting his fellow tribesmen, and so can accrue power, prestige, and loyalty.

Besides the 'āqila and the rajal khair, there exist two external roles which form part of the total system of Bedouin authority. The roles of 'umda and shaikh are defined as political offices, but function more as structural aspects of the Egyptian governmental authority structure. The roles were created and imposed upon the Bedouin by Muḥammad 'Ali during the early part of the nineteenth century in order to facilitate administration, maintain security in the desert, and protect the western frontier. Both roles are representative at the primary level of the tribal structure. Thus the 'Aishaibāt have an 'umda and a shaikh who reside in Marsa Maṭrūḥ and work in cooperation with the Governor of the desert province. The incumbents are answerable to both the Governor and the Bedouin, and no real decision-making power resides with them. Since they have no traditional basis of authority, they can make no decisions which are morally binding for the Bedouin.

The political roles discussed represent a struggle over the distribution of power and authority in the desert. At the heart of this struggle is the role of rajal khair. Traditionally, the rajal khair has faced inward and outward. He has capitalized on his traditional prestige to augment his external status and influence. At the same time, his economic qualifications have led him naturally toward the market Marsa Maṭrūḥ. In the present stage of transition, the rajal khair is in a position to combine his ascribed and achieved attributes most effectively. This affords him new opportunities for power--perhaps even authority--over his fellow Bedouin. The rajal khair maintains a _tertium quid_ status. He has one foot in the traditional community and the other in the modern camp. He is able to enter into dialogue with the modern because his "status honor" renders him public recognition at the local institutional level. It would seem that the rajal khair, who is neither an 'āqila nor an 'umda, is in a favorable structural and ideological position to assume leadership during the period of transition. It is possible that in the future a new role will emerge. This is what I wish to explore in the "case study" which follows.

Ḥajj Mukhaḍram: A Case Study

Ḥajj Mukhaḍram* is a very prestigious member of the "status group" by virtue of his wealth and family. He has elevated his "status honor" through the role of the rajal khair. He has mustered local support and debts as a consequence. Further, he has demonstrated his "superiority" by excelling in the outside business world. He has done all this while remaining a "good Bedouin" in the traditional sense of the word.

Ḥajj Mukhaḍram actively seeks to be a leader among the Bedouin. He is looking for a place in the central governmental structure, though he has refused the position of 'āqila. He will not be bound by an authority role, and seeks power outside his local community. The political position Ḥajj Mukhaḍram seeks is that of a "cultural broker."

Ḥajj Mukhaḍram belongs to one of the two most powerful lineages in the desert. He is fifty-three years old. He has

---

*Ḥajj Mukhaḍram is a pseudonym, but a particularly apt one for a Bedouin in transition. Wehr's _A Dictionary of Modern Written Arabic_ (1966) defines _mukhaḍram_ as a "designation of such contemporaries of Muḥammad, esp. of poets, whose life span bridges the time of paganism and that of Islam; an old man who has lived through several generations or historical epochs."

been married five times, divorced once, and at present has four wives. All of these marriages have served economic and political purposes. In each case, a wife is from a lineage holding land contiguous to his own property, or from the other most powerful 'Aishaibi lineage. All of the marriages are alliances which increase the social status and political power of Ḥajj Mukhaḍram.

Although he is without formal education, and can neither read nor write, Ḥajj Mukhaḍram has sent his son to the University of Alexandria--one of the few men of the desert to do so. He preferred that his son study law or enter the military academy and "become an officer," but his son objected, saying, "Either way I will be employed by the government and will not be permitted to travel and see other countries." The boy enrolled in the Faculty of Commerce. Ḥajj Mukhaḍram was also the first to enroll his daughters in the local primary school.

Ḥajj Mukhaḍram derives his wealth from a number of sources. Although he is now committed primarily to olive farming, he owns one of the largest herds of sheep in the tribe. Thus he is identified with both the old and the new symbols of status. He owns three small general stores operated mostly on a credit basis. Lineage members, as debtors, are both grateful and beholden to their kinsman and creditor. He is the only member of the 'Aishaibāt tribe who owns two or more shops, and the only Bedouin in the whole Western Desert who owns three shops. One shop is at the Libyan-Egyptian border--an "import-export" enterprise, among other things.

In addition to all this, Ḥajj Mukhaḍram is involved in a small stone-cutting operation supplying stones for house construction, cooperates with his three brothers in a well-cleaning business, and subcontracts government heavy equipment for excavation and building dams. His success and status is evident in the fact that he is the only man in the tribal area with two large compound-type houses, and the only man with four wives. He has also made the pilgrimage to Mecca twice, which entails considerable expense but contributes to accumulated status.

Ḥajj Mukhaḍram is the third party most frequently sought after in conflict situations. He is often asked to participate in political matters not only by the disputants themselves, but also by the 'āqila or other third party presiding. He is sometimes asked to be present as a witness for important contractual matters, such as agreements between 'awāqil.

Ḥajj Mukhaḍram, then, operates very effectively in the local micropolitical system. Equally important, he has secured a firm foothold in the modern bureaucratic structure of the provincial capital. He straddles both camps. (The Governor of Marsa Maṭrūḥ was an important aid to my understanding of Ḥajj

Mukhaḍram as a "broker." The Governor said that "this Bedouin" speaks well and thinks well, that he "became an 'āqila by his way of life." Of course, Ḥajj Mukhaḍram is not an 'aqila, but the Governor, as an outsider, understandably mistook such an influential leader as an 'āqilā.)

Other traits qualify Ḥajj Mukhaḍram as a singular leader of the 'Aishaibi Bedouin. A few years back, the Governor of Marsa Maṭrūḥ formed a Governor's Council (Majlis al-Muḥāfaza) made up of persons representing both the Western Desert Bedouin population and the government employees in the province. Ḥajj Mukhaḍram was one of the six men from his tribe appointed to the Council, and the only one without a formal political role. I attended one meeting of the Council, during which only the Governor and Egyptian officials took part in the discussion. At the conclusion of the meeting, the Governor asked for comments. Ḥajj Mukhaḍram arose and delivered a well-prepared speech concerning the inadequacies of the educational facilities in the town of Marsa Maṭrūḥ. He noted that the Governor had promised the Bedouin that if they sent their sons in from the desert for secondary schooling, the boys' material needs would be met, but that the Governor had not kept his promise, for there was not enough space and beds for the boys. The Governor apologized for these conditions and promised improvements. A few Egyptian officials smiled about the incident, but all of the Bedouin present nodded seriously in agreement with the points made by Ḥajj Mukhaḍram.

Ḥajj Mukhaḍram was the only Bedouin to speak up at this meeting. He spoke in the formal traditional manner and showed concern for the real problems of the Bedouin. Ḥajj Mukhaḍram is careful to protect his identity as a Bedouin; in this respect he differs from the 'umda and most others of the "status group." He is both an agent and a recipient of change, and is therefore intimate with the problems of the Bedouin. He is able to articulate the wants of his fellow tribesmen, and his place on the Governor's Council gives him the right and the opportunity to tender them. His formulation and presentation of demands linking the traditional and modern systems is a political process which Ḥajj Mukhaḍram manipulates in his role of "cultural broker."

Once each year the Governor makes a general inspection of the desert area. A local reception is held in a ceremonial tent set up for the occasion. During the visit, he makes his evaluations and states his opinions, distributes some clothing materials to the poorer families of the area, and asks for suggestions from the Bedouin who sit at his feet before the ceremonial tent. On one such occasion Ḥajj Mukhaḍram delivered an eloquent speech in which he made no requests but simply thanked the Governor for the honor of his presence. In his short tribute he said:

> We feel the efforts of the government, and we can scarcely dream of this development. We were living in tents, and now only five percent remain in tents while the remainder are in houses. We were dressed simply, but now we are dressed in fine material. Those who could afford one set of clothes can now afford two. Thanks be to God, all this is due to Jamal Abd al-Naṣṣer.

It is significant that once again there were droll smiles on the faces of the Governor's entourage, but only serious admiration on the faces of the Bedouin. As Ḥajj Mukhaḍram spoke, he turned aside, speaking both to the Governor and the tribesmen; Ḥajj Mukhaḍram--the Bedouin--had been sitting on the ground before the Governor. The 'umda and shaikh were seated on chairs inside the tent with other officials.

Ḥajj Mukhaḍram, being politically active and representative in both the traditional and modern political systems, seeks to change the old ways in the direction of the new. He is both conscious of traditions and nation-oriented at the same time. Ḥajj Mukhaḍram was the only man from the local area who was neither a shaikh nor an 'umda to attend the nomination of Jamal Abd al-Naṣṣer in 1965. He is committed to working closely with the Governor of Marsa Maṭrūḥ. (When I asked him to help me in my field study, he refused, saying, "You will have to bring me a letter from the Governor stating that he wishes me to cooperate with you.") His role identification as an agent of change is indicated in his remark "I have heard there are others in the desert who feel and think the way I myself do."

Ḥajj Mukhaḍram is discretely aware of the status difference between himself, as a member of the "status group," and others of the desert. I was invited to his house for _iid al-fitr_--the feast marking the end of Ramaḍān. After a surprisingly simple meal of bread, dates, peanuts, and tea, Ḥajj Mukhaḍram explained to me: "My neighbors do not have my economic advantages, and I do not think it is proper to serve other than what they eat." He is conscious of the social stratification in his society and empathizes with the lower ranks. Such awareness is a prerequisite for a traditional Bedouin leader, and an advantage for a modern leader.

The outstanding characteristic of Ḥajj Mukhaḍram is his sensitivity to the relationship between traditional institutions and the conditions of modernity. He sees only disadvantages in the structural pillars of Bedouin society. Concerning the tradition of cousin-right marriage he says:

> One thing which I do not like about our customs is the idea that a man has a right to his father's brother's daughter. The man binds his cousin and in the end he might not even

> marry her. He will be the cause of her never marrying. He gives himself the authority to decide whom she may or may not marry. If he knows she desires to marry a certain man, he says, "She can marry anyone but not that one."

It has been noted that the bait, as a political group, is structurally defined by the corporate principle resting upon collective responsibility in matters of compensation and blood-revenge. All of my informants, though they disagreed over the procedures of revenge, insisted that it was the inviolable right of the Arabs. But Hajj Mukhaḍram takes exception to the practice of blood-revenge for a number of reasons. He says:

> The world changes. Before it was only the 'awaiyid [customary law] and the Border Guards which kept order. The government should now enter into the matter of killings. Personally, I do not agree with the old custom and the way it operates. In the case of killing, for instance, someone who is not worth anything kills one from another tribe. Then the tribe of the killer asks for protection and a third party becomes involved. The third party agrees to guard the killer's bait for twelve months, and so the business of all those involved must stop. A member of the third party's family must accompany everywhere each member of the killer's tribe. But even after the twelve months, the tribe of the murdered man will try to avenge on the best man in the killer's tribe. How many good ones do we have in one tribe?

In questioning the right to blood-revenge, he challenges the structural basis of the group and, in effect, the very concept of traditional authority. He empathizes with the man in the third-party role and with the prominent man who becomes a primary target in matters of revenge.

Ḥajj Mukhaḍram is unhappy with yet another tenet of traditional society. Concerning the logic and authority for the oath as a sacred sanction, he says:

> I do not like the idea of swearing the oath. For instance, if I steal 1,000 pounds from you, then you will accuse me. The 'āqila will then come to me and say: "If you did not steal the money, swear the oath." Some of my family will support me in this, swearing that I did not steal the money. The swearing of the oath will take place at the tomb, in the presence of the Qurān. This tomb belongs to a dead man, and they tell you that he is a saint. First of all, the thief will always swear the oath and they will believe him, and, secondly, what is the sense of swearing in front of a dead body?

He makes no mention of the prevalent Bedouin belief that misfortune will befall the one who lies under oath.

Ḥajj Mukhaḍram actively challenges the old bases of the Bedouin moral and political community. Striving to do away with prescribed cousin-right in marriage, the mechanisms of blood-revenge, and the oath as a means of supporting law and order in the desert is what we would expect from an outside official embarked on a program to integrate the Bedouin into national society. In fact, these are all customs which the Governor of Marsa Maṭrūḥ believes must eventually be eradicated. It is not surprising that Ḥajj Mukhaḍram's son believes that "it is not civilized to lay claim to my cousin" for, like his father, he also is redefining morality with respect to "civilization."

If Ḥajj Mukhaḍram is to legitimate his own authority in a new political system, he must show the Bedouin the legitimacy of new political symbols and meanings which are the basis of developing a moral commitment toward a new national community. The majority of Bedouin unconsciously feel that the traditional allocation of political values and distribution of power will be carried over into the modern community. Most of them see change coming, but do not see it as any threat to the traditional order of things. Thus since the 'umda represents them at the local provincial level, he should do the same in the National Assembly in Cairo.

Ḥajj Mukhaḍram anticipates the change as so fundamental as to require a new sense of identity. He takes issue with traditional patterns and appears to anticipate the emergence of a new role:

> There is another objection which I have concerning our customs. I mean the case of elections. For instance, one from the 'Aishaibāt and one from the Sanagra are nominated. Then each man must vote for the one from his own tribe. He must vote for the 'Aishaibi even if the other is the best man. But we should consider that the best man is the man with the best qualifications. 'Umda Khalil, for instance, knows how to greet an official or a minister, but he does not know the 'awaiyid or the problems of the Bedouin. His brother, who will probably be the next 'umda, is a good man and is educated, but he does not know the 'awaiyid either.

Ḥajj Mukhaḍram is modern in his evaluation of the political situation, and knows the problems of his constituents. Although he is critical of Bedouin customary law, he feels one must know and understand it to change it. Through his negative appraisal of the 'umda, he implies that he himself is capable of understanding and, therefore, leading the Bedouin during the period of transition. His thoughtful statements about the transition also suggest this:

> The Bedouin need many things. We need factories as in the Nile Valley. For the desert, in particular, we need olive

> presses. This will raise the profits of the farmer. . . . We need a factory for canning tomatoes. The whole desert plants tomatoes, and the transportation is such that we cannot get them to the market in good time. . . . A cause of change here is the fact that everyone watches his neighbor. He sees what he does and he imitates him. Today I listen to the radio and tomorrow my neighbor buys one. Evolution (taṭawwur) is taking place and the people here are realistic about it. For instance, I do not know reading and writing, but my son knows better than I, just as I know better than my father did. He lived here for thirty-five years without knowing anything about the streets of Marsa Maṭrūḥ.

Elaborating on the role of education, Ḥajj Mukhaḍram shows insight into some of the psychological factors accompanying social change:

> As I said before, the people here are realistic about change. Now there are only about three or four of us who send our sons to study at the university. The rest of the people are waiting to see what these boys will amount to. The other day, one of our educated boys--an officer in the army--came for a visit. All of the women are now hoping to see their sons become as successful as this. This is exactly like the first time we planted olives in the desert. The Bedouins mocked those who cultivated the olive. After the olive began to show profits, everyone regretted that he did not plant it. Times are changing, and the people are changing. Education is the basis of everything in any nation. Now the agricultural engineer directs me, telling me what to do and how to do it. . . . And before 1952 [before 'Abd al-Naṣṣer] they knew nothing about us and we had nothing.

Ḥajj Mukhaḍram is the representative of this desert area to the Arab Socialist Union which holds its meetings in Marsa Maṭrūḥ. When I asked why Ḥajj Mukhaḍram spoke for the Bedouin at section meetings of the Union, the answer was: "Because he is a member of the Governor's Council." At one section meeting of the Union in 1965, the theme was "The Meaning of Socialism." Ḥajj Mukhaḍram participated in this meeting. All his political activities are beginning to converge--to crystallize in the form of a new role.

It seems not amiss to say that Ḥajj Mukhaḍram is prepared to take over the leadership of the Bedouin in a way more sophisticated than one usually expects in traditional politics. But Ḥajj Mukhaḍram, as everyone in the desert knows, is traditional and modern at the same time. He may not be educated, but he knows the 'awaiyid and stresses the fact that his son will have the education which he never had. Empathy is the primary trait and tool of the "cultural broker."

No one could explain to me why Ḥajj Mukhaḍram did not have an education, while all his brothers and most members of the "status group" read and write. Perhaps the transition itself is his stimulus. Ḥajj Mukhaḍram, the third party and "cultural broker," is politically conscious and creative in the context of two worlds in change--a last chance, conflict situation.

Footnotes

[1]Reinhard Bendix, Max Weber: An Intellectual Portrait (New York, 1962), p. 290.

[2]Max Weber, Economy and Society, 3 vols. (New York, 1968), p. 1414.

[3]David Easton, "Political Anthropology" in B. Siegel, ed., Biennial Review of Anthropology (Stanford, 1959).

[4]Ernest Gellner, Thought and Change (Chicago, 1964), p. 40.

[5]Claude Lévi-Strauss, "The Social and Psychological Aspects of Chieftainship in a Primitive Tribe: The Nambikuara of Northwestern Mato Grosso" in R. Cohen and L. Middleton, eds., Comparative Political Systems (New York, 1944), pp. 45-62.

[6]Eric Wolf, "Aspects of Group Relations in a Complex Society," American Anthropologist, 58, 1956, pp. 1065-1079.

[7]Ibid., pp. 1071-1072.

[8]Clifford Geertz, "The Javanese Kijaji: The Changing Role of a Cultural Broker," Comparative Studies in Society and History, 2, 1960, p. 229.

[9]Alexander Goldenweiser, "Loose Ends of Theory on the Individual, Pattern, and Involution in Primitive Society" in Essays in Anthropology Presented to A.L. Kroeber (Berkeley, 1936), p. 103.

[10]Emrys Peters, "Some Structural Aspects of Feud among the Bedouin of Cyrenaica," Africa, 37, 1967, pp. 262-282.

[11]M.G. Smith, "Segmentary Lineage Systems," Journal of the Royal Anthropological Institute, 86, 1956, pp. 39-80.

[12]Max Weber, The Theory of Social and Economic Organization, edited by Talcott Parsons. (New York, 1947), p. 145.

[13]Sir Henry Maine, Ancient Law (New York, 1917), p. 203.

[14] W. Robertson Smith, Kinship and Marriage in Early Arabia, rev. ed. (London, 1903).

[15] Peters, p. 280.

[16] H.H. Gerth and C. Wright Mills, From Max Weber: Essays in Sociology (New York, 1946), pp. 186-300.

[17] S.N. Eisenstadt, Essays on Comparative Institutions (New York, 1965), p. 30.

[18] Peters, p. 145.

INSTITUTE OF INTERNATIONAL STUDIES
UNIVERSITY OF CALIFORNIA, BERKELEY

CARL G. ROSBERG,
Director

Monographs published by the Institute include:

RESEARCH SERIES

1. *The Chinese Anarchist Movement*, by Robert A. Scalapino and George T. Yu. ($1.00)
6. *Local Taxation in Tanganyika*, by Eugene C. Lee. ($1.00)
7. *Birth Rates in Latin America: New Estimates of Historical Trends*, by O. Andrew Collver. ($2.50)
12. *Land Tenure and Taxation in Nepal*, Volume IV, *Religious and Charitable Land Endowments: Guthi Tenure*, by Mahesh C. Regmi. ($2.75)
13. *The Pink Yo-Yo: Occupational Mobility in Belgrade, ca 1915-1965*, by Eugene A. Hammel. ($2.00)
14. *Community Development in Israel and the Netherlands: A Comparative Analysis*, by Ralph M. Kramer. ($2.50)

*15. *Central American Economic Integration: The Politics of Unequal Benefits*, by Stuart I. Fagan. ($2.00)

16. *The International Imperatives of Technology: Technological Development and the International Political System*, by Eugene B. Skolnikoff. ($2.95)

*17. *Autonomy or Dependence as Regional Integration Outcomes: Central America*, by Philippe C. Schmitter. ($1.75)

18. *Framework for a General Theory of Cognition and Choice*, by R.M. Axelrod. ($1.50)
19. *Entry of New Competitors in Yugoslav Market Socialism*, by S.R. Sacks. ($2.50)

*20. *Political Integration in French-Speaking Africa*, by Abdul A. Jalloh. ($3.50)

21. *The Desert and the Sown: Nomads in the Wider Society*, ed. by Cynthia Nelson. ($3.50)
22. *U.S.-Japanese Competition in International Markets: A Study of the Trade-Investment Cycle in Modern Capitalism*, by John E. Roemer. ($3.95)
23. *Political Disaffection Among British University Students: Concepts, Measurement, and Causes*, by Jack Citrin and David J. Elkins. ($2.00)
24. *Urban Inequality and Housing Policy in Tanzania: The Problem of Squatting*, by Richard E. Stren. ($2.50)

*25. *The Obsolescence of Regional Integration Theory*, by Ernst B. Haas. ($2.95)

26. *The Voluntary Service Agency in Israel*, by Ralph M. Kramer. ($2.00)
27. *The SOCSIM Demographic-Sociological Microsimulation Program: Operating Manual*, by Eugene A. Hammel et al. ($4.50)
28. *Authoritarian Politics in Communist Europe: Uniformity & Diversity in One-Party States*, ed. by Andrew C. Janos. ($3.95)
29. *The Anglo-Icelandic Cod War of 1972-1973: A Case Study of a Fishery Dispute*, by Jeffrey A. Hart. ($2.00)
30. *Plural Societies and New States: A Conceptual Analysis*, by Robert Jackson. ($2.00)
31. *The Politics of Crude Oil Pricing in the Middle East, 1970-1975: A Study in International Bargaining*, by Richard Chadbourn Weisberg. ($3.95)
32. *Agricultural Policy and Performance in Zambia: History, Prospects, and Proposals for Change*, by Doris Jansen Dodge. ($4.95)
33. *Five Classy Programs: Computer Procedures for the Classification of Households*, by E.A. Hammel and R.Z. Deuel. ($3.75)
34. *Housing the Urban Poor in Africa: Policy, Politics, and Bureaucracy in Mombasa*, by Richard E. Stren. ($5.95)
35. *The Russian New Right: Right-Wing Ideologies in the Contemporary USSR*, by Alexander Yanov. ($4.50)

*International Integration Series

INSTITUTE OF INTERNATIONAL STUDIES MONOGRAPHS (continued)

36. *Social Change in Romania, 1860-1940: A Debate on Development in a European Nation*, ed. by Kenneth Jowitt. ($4.50)
37. *The Leninist Response to National Dependency*, by Kenneth Jowitt. ($3.25)
38. *Socialism in Sub-Saharan Africa: A New Assessment*, ed. by Carl G. Rosberg and Thomas M. Callaghy. ($9.50)
39. *Tanzania's Ujamaa Villages: The Implementation of a Rural Development Strategy*, by Dean E. McHenry, Jr. ($5.95)
40. *Who Gains from Deep Ocean Mining? Simulating the Impact of Regimes for Regulating Nodule Exploitation*, by I.G. Bulkley. ($3.50)
41. *Industrialization, Industrialists, and the Nation-State in Peru: A Comparative/Sociological Analysis*, by Frits Wils. ($5.95)
42. *Ideology, Public Opinion, and Welfare Policy: Attitudes toward Taxes and Spending in Industrialized Societies*, by Richard M. Coughlin. ($4.95)
43. *The Apartheid Regime: Political Power and Racial Domination*, ed. by Robert M. Price and Carl G. Rosberg. ($8.95)
44. *The Yugoslav Economic System and Its Performance in the 1970s*, by Laura D'Andrea Tyson. ($4.50)

POLITICS OF MODERNIZATION SERIES

1. *Spanish Bureaucratic-Patrimonialism in America*, by Magali Sarfatti. ($2.00)
2. *Civil-Military Relations in Argentina, Chile, and Peru*, by Liisa North. ($2.00)
3. *Notes on the Process of Industrialization in Argentina, Chile, and Peru*, by Alcira Leiserson. ($1.75)
6. *Modernization and Coercion*, by Mario Barrera. ($1.50)
8. *Developmental Processes in Chilean Local Government*, by Peter S. Cleaves. ($1.50)
9. *Modernization and Bureaucratic-Authoritarianism: Studies in South American Politics*, by Guillermo A. O'Donnell. ($5.50)

POLICY PAPERS IN INTERNATIONAL AFFAIRS

1. *Images of Detente and the Soviet Political Order*, by Kenneth Jowitt. ($1.25)
2. *Detente After Brezhnev: The Domestic Roots of Soviet Foreign Policy*, by Alexander Yanov. ($3.00)
3. *The Mature Neighbor Policy: A New United States Economic Policy for Latin America*, by Albert Fishlow. ($2.00)
4. *Five Images of the Soviet Future: A Critical Review and Synthesis*, by George W. Breslauer. ($2.50)
5. *Global Evangelism Rides Again: How to Protect Human Rights Without Really Trying*, by Ernst B. Haas. ($2.00)
6. *Israel and Jordan: Implications of an Adversarial Partnership*, by I. Lustick ($2.00)
7. *Political Syncretism in Italy: Historical Coalition Strategies and the Present Crisis*, by Giuseppe Di Palma. ($2.00)
8. *U.S. Foreign Policy in Sub-Saharan Africa: National Interest and Global Strategy*, by Robert M. Price. ($2.25)
9. *East-West Technology Transfer in Perspective*, by R.J. Carrick. ($2.75)
10. *NATO's Unremarked Demise*, by Earl C. Ravenal. ($2.00)
11. *Toward an Africanized U.S. Policy for Southern Africa: A Strategy for Increasing Political Leverage*, by Ronald T. Libby. ($3.95)
12. *The Taiwan Relations Act and the Defense of the Republic of China*, by Edwin K. Snyder et al. ($3.95)
13. *Cuba's Policy in Africa, 1959-1980*, by William M. LeoGrande. ($3.25)

Address correspondence to:

Institute of International Studies
215 Moses Hall
University of California
Berkeley, California 94720